THE TRUTH
ABOUT
ENLIGHTENMENT

THE TRUTH ABOUT ENLIGHTENMENT

HOW TO FIND EGOLESSNESS, NONDUALITY, AND WISDOM ON THE BUDDHIST PATH

Fred H. Meyer, MD

ISBN Paperback: 978-1-7365157-1-6

Library of Congress Control Number: 2021904659

Printed in the United States of America.

Fred H. Meyer, MD
www.fredhmeyermd.com

I dedicate this book to my wife Arla. I would never have lived to write it without her loving and steadfast care during a long illness.

CONTENTS

THE TRUTH ABOUT ENLIGHTENMENT

INTRODUCTION

This book is about enlightenment and how to experience it. *Enlightenment* is a word used to describe the pinnacle of human experience, as discovered by Gautama Buddha 2,500 years ago, and as experienced by the great teachers who followed him up to the present time. To become enlightened is to have insight into the true nature of mind and reality. Stated simply, that nature is emptiness inseparable from awareness. What those words mean, and, more importantly, how they feel, is the basis of this book.

To understand enlightenment intellectually helps us, but the real purpose of the Buddhist path is to experience enlightenment ourselves. Unfortunately, any effort to attain this experience poses a problem, because it is unworkable trying to be the enlightenment we already are, but have yet to appreciate. Our real nature will always be distorted by any attempts to find it.

Still, we must discover a way to realize our greatest human attribute. This book provides that, by outlining the progressive steps in insight required to travel the path to enlightenment, and the obstacles we must overcome in order to realize those insights. It also reveals how each insight actually feels, and how to know that what we feel is authentic. It concludes with a detailed description of the supports we need to travel the Buddhist path to enlightenment. These closing sections are well worth reviewing at any point on the path, but they will be particularly helpful for newer practitioners.

Words can never fully impart any experience, and certainly not enlightenment. What this book provides, however, is the truth about enlightenment and how to realize it. If we follow its recommendations, we will place ourselves in the best position to succeed in attaining enlightenment. And if we do, we will experience complete freedom, bliss, peace and restfulness, uncontrived compassion, and an understanding of the true nature of reality. In short, we will have discovered the best use of our human existence.

Although confusion abounds in the spiritual marketplace, you will not find obfuscating words and ideas here. Through effort, an incomparable teacher, and a good deal of luck, I have become the experiences I describe in this book. Moreover, the guidelines I offer do not differ in any way from the teachings of the spiritual masters who have attained enlightenment through the millennia. The insights recounted here, and the practices that lead to them, are authentic. If you follow them, they guarantee that you will understand and remain on the path to enlightenment.

INTRODUCING INSIGHT

1

CAUGHT BETWEEN

Traveling the Buddhist path is difficult, and traveling to its fruition—enlightenment—is especially so. Most practitioners find themselves "caught between" on the journey: knowing that fruition exists, but unable to reach it.

Fortunately, the path brings benefits at every stage. Through years of training, most of us learn to notice our mental impulses, such as anger or wanting, without being carried away by full-blown emotional upheavals. As such, we are calmer, and more aware of the workings of our own and others' minds. Along with this increased understanding, our commitment to work for the benefit of others has taken root, and we treat people more considerately and deal with unpleasant interactions more skillfully. By adhering to the Buddhist lay precepts (not to steal, lie, kill, commit sexual misdeeds, or misuse alcohol or drugs), we also reduce chaos in our lives, and the lives of those around us. We are also less goal-oriented in our meditation practice, and less likely to cloud our minds by seeking after results such as peace, joy, or enlightenment.

Despite these benefits, almost all of us remain caught between knowing that enlightenment exists, and not being able to experience it. Our practice has shown us much about the *activities* of mind, such as thoughts and emotions, but it has yet to reveal the mind those activities occur in.

When we read or hear teachings, we understand the concepts and the various practice instructions, but we still find the words pointing to major insights mystifying. If someone puts us on the spot by asking, "What is emptiness?" or "What is the experience of one taste?" we feel inadequate or threatened.

We may even have some personal insight into the absence of self, also known as egolessness of self, and may believe we are enlightened, especially if we don't read the teachings or have access to an authentic teacher. This misperception can seriously impede further insight on the path.

In general, most of us, lacking insight, will be practicing various types of personality adjustment: trying to be more mindful, disciplined in word and deed, or humble. Despite our best efforts, though, we continue to feel the strain of these personality adjustments, and others notice it as well. It is inescapable that any process of *trying* to be what we think we should be will fail the test of time. Our aggression, self-centeredness, or other habitual tendencies invariably overwhelm our best attempts to be "good little boys and girls," as my teacher once labeled self-improvement types.

I am reminded of a reputable Tibetan teacher who gave a talk I attended. At the talk, the sound system was performing poorly, and it became apparent that the teacher was not pleased with the sound system and the people operating it. His position would not allow him to show overt anger, so he was caught between his anger and repressing it, and the stress became quite apparent. I learned later that he had anger issues and struck his students. Personality adjustment, without the benefit of insight, will invariably break down.

Since enlightenment is rare, students who are caught between also find ways to justify their failure to attain it. A common belief, whether overt or tacit, is that only people with robes and religious titles can attain enlightenment, and that it is beyond the abilities of lay students. This attitude makes insight a taboo topic in lay communal settings, where practitioners who bring it up are branded as presumptuous, arrogant, or deluded. Students even doubt the very existence of enlightenment, because they have never witnessed it, having never been in the presence of a realized teacher.

Compassion is warranted for those students who find ways to undermine the fruitions of the path, because enlightenment is difficult enough without denying its very existence. I remember spending a period with an excellent Zen teacher, Kobun Chino (who did not use honorifics like *sensei* or *roshi*). I once asked him why a teacher named Yasutani Roshi had broken away from Soto Zen. He replied that Yasutani had done so because, in Yasutani's experience, there was "no enlightenment" in Soto Zen. Soto is a huge sect of Zen Buddhism with a long, impressive history, so I was surprised and saddened by this comment.

Although practicing the Dharma (Buddhist way) always brings benefit, I still find it tragic to contemplate the millions of students who devote their lives to enlightenment, and do not attain it. How many caught-between students faithfully follow the Buddhist tradition for their whole lives, without ever experiencing its crowning insight? In the following chapters, we will learn in detail what that insight is, and how to improve our chances of attaining it.

2

WHAT INSIGHTS ARE

Mahayana Buddhism, the tradition of practices and teachings devoted to helping others, has an approach to enlightenment called the *six paramitas*. The Sanskrit term *paramitas* is translated as "activities that take us to the other shore"—meaning that they help us cross the turbulent waters of confused mind, and reach the shore of enlightenment. The first five paramitas (generosity, discipline, patience, exertion, and meditative concentration) are skillful means. By applying them in daily life, we become more gentle, caring, and alert in ways that help ourselves and others.

The sixth paramita is *prajña*: transcendental insight. Prajña is crucial, because no matter how great our commitment to the first five paramitas, without prajña the crossing to enlightenment is impossible. Without it, our best efforts will always be subverted by ego.

11

This ego-centered pattern holds throughout our Buddhist journey. We can make some gains through behavioral adjustment, but to fundamentally progress in the Dharma requires insights that reveal *the view*, the true nature of mind. As Lodro Thaye writes:

The one who meditates without the view

Is like a blind man wandering the plains.

There is no reference point for where the true path is.

The Rain of Wisdom, 84.

What are insights? Quite simply, they are experiences, just like riding a bike, petting a horse, or flying a plane. And as with those activities, the experiences themselves are far removed from how we might imagine them to be. Furthermore, each insight illuminates more clearly what we are (or aren't), and how the world really *is*. Also, no one "has" these experiences: they are experiences without an experiencer. (The following chapters will address that seeming absurdity.)

Once seen, insights never leave. This is especially important to remember, because many feelings arise in life and meditation, some of them impressively lucid or pleasurable. Nevertheless, if they are transitory, they are not true insight. These transitory experiences are known in Tibetan as *nyam*.

We must not attach to nyam or seek their recurrence, but simply treat them as we treat all occurrences of mind and allow them to proceed on their way. I remember on several occasions entering nature after prolonged meditation, and being overwhelmed by its vividness and beauty. After one solitary retreat, I awoke to a fresh Vermont snowfall in full sunlight sparkling on the ground and trees, and the beauty stopped my mind. Another time at a Buddhist seminary, I was riveted by a river edged in ice that had become me. Its sounds were me, the sharply detailed borders of the ice were me, and the bubbles caught under the ice were me. They were who I was. What I saw in both instances resulted from the clearing of my mind by meditation, and not from true insight. I had been "close," but I had still not crossed the fine line of conceptualization that separated me from true reality. As a result, these experiences, like all nyam, did not persist.

Profound insights into reality are difficult to realize, because we have obstacles so deeply ingrained in us that we don't even know they exist. For example, how many of us would suspect that we had no self, if we had never heard or read of that possibility? Even if we had, how many would accept such a proposition, so completely outside our sense of reality? We live in a world that believes in self, and we act on that basis, working to become a success, undermine our enemies, and ignore what doesn't fit our plans. How many of us truly see the errors in that ego-driven approach? And this is just one of many reflexive beliefs that obscure our mind to enlightenment.

I had the greatest fortune possible in meeting a Buddha in my lifetime. From time to time when I was in his presence, he would reveal to me the enlightened nature of my mind. I would then enter a paradise, which was vivid, spacious, and in which my hopes and fears dissolved and I became completely free. Nevertheless, I had one prevalent obstacle: doubt. Time and again, I would begin to doubt something or someone, and it would take over my mind and erase paradise. During one of these experiences, I even doubted the authenticity of my teacher, who was providing the insight. I looked suspiciously into his eyes—and entered what felt like a vast, empty room with sterile white walls. This room was so devoid of anything to be suspicious of—and so boring in comparison to my usually clamorous and churning mind—that my doubt stopped immediately, and I remained in realization a bit longer. This was just one fault of the many thousands my mind is capable of, and which excluded me from staying in enlightenment. It's easy to see from this example how difficult it is to transcend mind's myriad obstacles.

Even for those of us with excellent Buddhist training, impediments to insight occur. One is failing to apply the supports on the path to enlightenment. Unless they are monastics, many Buddhists feel that they don't have time to practice or study the Dharma, because of family and work commitments, illnesses, and the other occurrences of life. It is not easy handling the stresses of everyday life and maintaining a meditative mind without a committed Dharma practice.

Another major problem, especially in the West, is entertainment. When the great Tibetan Nyingma master Dilgo Khyentse Rinpoche visited the United States, he met an American who expressed his excitement that the popularity of the Dharma here would certainly mean many enlightened Americans. Khyentse Rinpoche had his doubts, however, and through his translator said, "Too much entertainment." This was some time ago; one wonders what his response would be to the arrival of social media.

Knowing the significant difficulty in attaining insight, what can we do to realize it? First, as with scientific breakthroughs, insight occurs to the prepared mind. In Buddhism, a prepared mind knows the teachings. Also, a prepared mind notices what it experiences, because practice lessens its incessant stream of mental occurrences, and leaves room for it to see what arises. If we want to see a particular tree, it is easier to appreciate it in a meadow than in a forest.

Also, over time, practitioners learn that we cannot manufacture realization—so we stop trying. That opens our minds more, allowing insights to occur spontaneously; and, without exception, that's how they do occur. We can't manufacture or figure out intuition. The teachings play a role as well, alerting us to what to expect and preventing us from going astray.

Finally, an authentic teacher may directly point out insights, sometimes wordlessly. The very special ones display realization in everything they do. Simply remembering how precisely my teacher did and said things continues to remind me of the true nature of mind, many years after I last saw him.

This has been a general introduction to Buddhist insights, the obstacles to attaining them, and how we can overcome those obstacles. Now we will discuss in sequence the major insights in Buddhism, and how they lead to enlightenment. We will begin with the discovery that there has never been, is not now, and will never be a self.

Major Insights on
the Path

3

Egolessness of Self

At this point, we turn to discussing the actual insights that arise on the path to enlightenment. The first of these is egolessness of self, or the absence of self.

Let's first clarify what we mean by "self." Self is a feeling that there is someone inside us that is who we are, someone who does our thinking, feels our emotions, runs our life, and is the center of our world. We most easily recognize it by its wanting; it wants incessantly, much like a baby consumed by its own needs.

Self is what feels discomfort or uneasiness when entering a group, seeking a job, or being made fun of. We can experience it quite clearly in conversations with certain types of people, who talk exclusively about their own successes or problems.

"Self" is often used synonymously with "ego," and hence the topic of this chapter refers rather awkwardly to the selflessness of self. "Self" can be used in other ungainly ways as well. For example, in some spiritual disciplines, "self" denotes the self inside us in one context, and the totality of insight in another. This double usage leads to statements like, "One must transcend the self to understand the Self." To promote clarity, "self" is better confined to the sense of something inside us, and other words used for spiritual revelations. Discussing gnosis is difficult enough without using the same word to describe contrasting experiences.

Egolessness of self is simply the realization of the absence, or nonexistence, of self. That absence manifests as a new space inside of us where ego used to be, and that space, once experienced, never leaves. The sign of egolessness of self is that we no longer experience any entity having our thoughts, emotions, or any other of life's experiences.

Egolessness of self can appear in an instant, as happened to me in my late thirties, when, quite stressed over work, I sat on my bed and asked myself, "What are you going to do, Fred?" Looking at whom I was addressing, I was surprised to find no one.

Fortunately, I had been introduced to Zen Buddhism and had met a teacher, studied the teachings, and meditated, so I recognized what had happened. As to how it happened, I sometimes addressed myself for various reasons. If I felt threatened by life, I would tell myself to be courageous, and if things were going well, I might congratulate myself for my successes. I never realized that what I said to myself was not nearly as important as looking inside for the respondent.

Looking inside is a practice in Buddhism. Sitting meditation has an element of it, and there is also a more explicit tradition of directing practitioners to look for who is having their thoughts and emotions. Most of us believe it's "ourselves," but if we continue to search for the source of mind's occurrences, we may one day realize that they come not from ego, but from nowhere. That is the experience of egolessness of self.

Another enabling factor for the insight was my own total lack of expectation. Most of the time, I paid little attention to self; it had always been there, and I had no reason to expect it would suddenly leave. If I had been seeking self's absence, it never would have happened, because the seeking would have been ego-driven. Looking does not involve ego unless we are looking *for* something—or for nothing—so when we look, we must do so simply, without expectations.

Lastly, on this occasion I had relaxed right before looking inside, and that relaxation played a role as well. Whether it made my mind clearer, loosened my sense of self, or both, I don't know, but it helped.

Egolessness of self is not always a single, sudden epiphany like mine. Some students have the experience over a longer period, a process that has been likened to wearing out a shoe by walking in it. Still other practitioners realize non-self through direct contact with a master. The Zen literature contains many stories of teachers bringing students to the understanding of no-self. In one instance, a master asked a student, "Who is it that carries your corpse around?" The student looked, and saw what I saw. This, and other Zen questions like it, are intended specifically to encourage the acolyte to look inside and see that no one is there. Another Zen method is to give students a mental chore that exhausts their intellect, like a koan to ponder or a saying to repeat. Masters might answer a question like "Why did Bodhidharma come from the west?"—meaning "Why did Bodhidharma bring enlightenment here?"—with "The cypress tree in the garden," or the query "Does a dog have Buddha nature?" with "Mu!" These koans exhaust students' intellectual searching, and cause them to give up and see the nothing that is left.

Like all insights, egolessness of self is difficult to realize. One reason for this difficulty is that ego arises as a series of extremely rapid steps that solidly establish its existence. These steps are the five *skandhas* (Sanskrit, "heaps"): *form, feeling, perception, formation* and *consciousness.* We experience them because of the aloneness and anxiety we feel when nothingness, our true state, emerges. Our immediate reaction to that feeling is the first skandha, *form,* a "negative miracle" of mind that manages to freeze limitless space into form. Next is a *feeling* of what form is, which reinforces its existence. Next is an attempt to create order in the new world of form and feeling with *perception*, which categorizes experience into names.

The first three skandhas are instinctual. Now, with the fourth, we volitionally begin the *formation* of re-actions to what we perceive—for example, disliking the color purple—further strengthening our sense of the perceiver or ego. Finally, to keep what has been created entertained, we play it mind movies, the *consciousness* of thoughts and emotions. That is how self is formed in a split second, as a response to our discomfort with nothingness.

Situations enhance and strengthen ego, as well. As we mentioned in the fourth skandha, we take stances on the world's occurrences. Instead of simply recognizing them as events occurring in limitless space, inseparable from mind, we now make them reference points that reinforce ego's credibility. Also, languages contain words like "I" or "me," and may be (like English) very ego-oriented in their grammar, all of which subtly reinforces the speaker's sense of self. Similarly, children learn early on about their self, and how smart, beautiful, or adorable it is. Later on, the media chips in to remind us that we are not attractive, successful, or productive enough. For these reasons and many others, seeing the nonexistence of ego is a challenge.

These challenges notwithstanding, when we do realize egolessness of self, the newfound freedom brings a sense of great joy and power. The joy comes from feeling as though the dictator that has ruled our life is deposed, and that we no longer have him or her looking over our shoulder. The power originates from the energy previously siphoned off for ego's needs being set free. In my case, the sense of power was so great that I sat on a levee in New Orleans and considered if I should destroy a bridge with my mind. I decided it would be cruel to do so, and dropped the idea. (To be clear: No, I couldn't have.)

These initial fireworks of non-self dissipate over time, and eventually the insight makes relatively little difference in our lives. We do not, for example, simply stop and stand gazing vacantly into space like the Energizer Bunny without a battery, as some suppose. In fact, we act much as we did when we had an ego. This is due partly to old habits, and partly to the fact that, even though we are different, the world remains the same. Our attentiveness to others and to life itself does improve somewhat, because self no longer diverts our attention. We also begin to realize that we are not our reference points, and that having a name, a job, or a car no longer defines what is no longer there.

By realizing egolessness of self, we take the first real step on the path to enlightenment, by seeing the first in the string of absences that will eventually become limitless space. Moreover, with this insight we enter the Dharma experientially, and discover that what we have heard is unquestionably true. We see what the Buddha saw 2,500 years ago, and what has been passed down to us through the lineages to the present day. We now know in our bones that the Dharma is valid, and that everything we've read and heard has a basis in experience. Furthermore, what we have seen can never not be seen, so it will always be with us.

Non-self is not a big step, but it is a critical one, because it takes us from the realm of belief to the realm of direct experience, the *sine qua non* of Buddhism. It also prepares us for egolessness of other, the next step on the path to enlightenment.

4

EGOLESSNESS
OF OTHER

Just as most of us believe in a self, we also believe that the world is real. When we look at a tree or a lake, we never question its reality, its authenticity, its existential validity. Our certainty is mistaken, however, and to correct our mistake, we must realize the next insight on the Buddhist path: egolessness of other.

Egolessness of other reveals that the world is unreal, and that worldly objects are illusions—like reflections in a mirror, mirages, or rainbows. The objects are called *egoless*, because seeing them correctly reveals them to lack inherent existence. That lack is the second absence on the path to enlightenment.

I first witnessed egolessness of other in my mid-fifties while taking a shower. I was completely brokenhearted over politics in the sangha (Buddhist community), and for a second I gave up—completely. We've all given up over situations, and I had at various points as well. This time, though, because of the overwhelming heartbreak, I let *everything* go, and in that moment I saw the nothingness that was left. It felt like a drawer suddenly opened, and when I looked in, nothing was there.

My teacher, Chögyam Trungpa Rinpoche, summarizes nicely what happened:

The contrast between such immense grasping, and such immense loss of that grasping, brings about a sense of loss, but a sense of gain at the same time. *1976 Hinayana-Mahayana Seminary Transcripts.*

What I lost was attachment, and what I gained was nothingness. In the same instant in which I saw nothingness, the world also became unreal, without inherent existence, and it has remained that way since. Fifteen years after realizing egolessness of self, I had experienced the truth of egolessness of other. I had waited fifteen years for what happened in an instant.

The insight did not have the pyrotechnics of egolessness of self, but the result was as profound.

From then on, buildings, bridges, and mountains appeared lighter, less solid, and less authoritative. That allowed me to relax, free from the intimidation of reality. It was as though I left a busy city street, entered a theater, and began watching a movie.

Common misconceptions exist about egolessness of other. First, to experience the illusoriness of phenomena does not mean that phenomena lose their conventional properties. Objects still have the physical qualities of an object; if we punch a wall, it hurts. (And while accounts exist of great teachers walking through them, I have yet to see it.) Also, when the world loses its realness, it becomes *more* vivid, rather than disappearing or somehow growing dull as some might imagine.

A more dangerous misconception is to mistake experiencing egolessness of other for experiencing enlightenment. If seeing the absence of self can falsely convince people they are enlightened, the impact of realizing that the world is unreal can *really* convince them. That is unfortunate, because there's still a long way to go on the path. A dead giveaway is that we now have two egolessnesses—of self, and of other—and the Dharma does not do twos, only ones or nones. When two exist, they interact with each other in sometimes painful ways, and so at this stage of insight we'll know we're not enlightened when we feel the psychological heat of passion, aggression, and ignorance as the two egolessnesses rub together.

What does a practitioner need to do to experience egolessness of other? I mentioned the fifteen-year gap in my own life, but I didn't describe what happened during that time. Those events may explain how I had the insight.

Most importantly, I met a Buddha, Chögyam Trungpa Rinpoche. Because I saw early on that he was enlightened, I followed to the letter all of his teachings, as well as his private guidance in my life. Also, I began doing more advanced practices in Vajrayana Buddhism, and some of those practices involved egolessness of other. As an example, visualizing a deity is seeing an unreal entity that is still there, exactly like perceiving an object in the world after the insight of egolessness of other. As such, the practice prepares one's mind for the insight.

During those years, I also joined a sangha, and had the benefit of living in a meditation center for several years, where I practiced daily and did numerous prolonged meditation retreats. I don't know what role those various activities played in my experiencing egolessness of other, but they couldn't have hurt.

I also believe that my teacher and his lineage helped me. For a non-Vajrayana practitioner, the idea of lineage can be difficult to comprehend. The thought of a line of enlightened beings extending back through millennia helping a student in the present day may sound like another item of religious dogma, a tendency to attribute everything good to some preordained beneficent entity.

In my experience, lineage is not dogma. I can remember several occasions where I saw paintings of my teacher's lineage and felt a spontaneous and unexpected sense of richness and devotion. I never abandoned my teacher and his lineage—even through very trying times in the sangha that gave me compelling reasons to do so—and my experience of egolessness of other may have arisen as a result. The writings of previous masters support this possibility, such as Lodro Thaye's *Song of Lodro Thaye*:

When you intensify devotion in your heart

Rock meets bone in insight

And the ultimate lineage blessing is received.

The Rain of Wisdom, 86.

Regardless of these preparations, to experience the unreality of the world, like all major insights on the path, is difficult to accomplish—above all, because we can't do it. A slogan in Mahayana Buddhism extolls practitioners to "Regard all dharmas as dreams," *dharmas* in this case being worldly occurrences. Although the Mahayana slogans have great merit, I have a problem with that particular one. If you'd like to become discouraged and maybe slightly crazy in a short period of time, then all you need to do is *try* and see everything you look at as a dream. If you perceive objects as being real, you can "regard" a tree however you like—look at it from any angle, squint, concentrate as much as possible—but nothing will change your perception. I know because I've tried. We can't force egolessness of other, or any insight; it has to happen, and how and when it happens is out of our control.

Another difficulty is that realizing egolessness of other usually follows realizing egolessness of self. That was the case in my teacher's presentation of the Dharma, and it was my own experience as well, which leads me to believe that attaining the second insight before the first is quite difficult.

Lastly, experiencing egolessness of other takes heart. By heart, I mean courage, will, dedication, and love. Up to this point, I have said little about heart, because non-self is generally something we simply see in an unguarded moment. Seeing is involved with egolessness of other also, but at this stage of the path it is heart that carries us through to realization.

Here, we need to commit our hearts completely—desperately—to enlightenment, realizing that there is no alternative for dealing with life. In my case, my commitment arose from the pain I felt practicing medicine, and my desire to transcend that pain so that I could continue to help others.

Another desperate person was Milarepa, who was haunted by having killed others with his magic, and who felt that enlightenment alone could relieve him of his guilt. One of Milarepa's nicknames was "the little man with the big heart," and he had courage and will so great that they overcame his mind's warnings about the risks he was taking in his quest for insight, even the risk of death. Ignoring your intelligence in that way is a recipe for disaster, which is exactly what Milarepa encountered.

Disaster appeared in the form of Marpa the Translator, a very tough, very insightful man who read Milarepa completely. Knowing that Milarepa was desperate for the teachings and why, and knowing the strength of Milarepa's heart, he decided that the way to bring him to insight was to break his heart by denying him the teachings. Marpa declared he would not teach Milarepa until he built him a stone tower, but during the tower's construction, Marpa would always find something wrong with it, and Milarepa would have to tear it down and start over. After eight attempts, Milarepa came to believe he would never get the teachings, even though his back was covered with infected sores from carrying rocks. His situation became so dire that he contemplated suicide, and others intervened on his behalf. That was a mistake. As Marpa revealed:

Had this son of mine completed nine ordeals, his complete Enlightenment, without future birth, would have been achieved without leaving any bodily residue.

The Life of Milarepa, 72.

Marpa had been prevented from breaking Milarepa's heart completely, and so Milarepa didn't have the chance to give up and tear away all that his heart was attached to—including things he never considered, like the reality of the world. At the level of egolessness of other, the Dharma becomes a business deal, where we get back what we invest. If we invest our whole heart in it, heartbreak tears all our attachments away, and our payout is nothingness, which reveals the world to be unreal. Milarepa missed the full payout on this occasion, but he made a complete withdrawal later.

At this point on the path, we have two absences: the absence that remains upon self's departure, and the world's absence of reality. Since twos are not part of the world of enlightenment, something must happen to make these two absences one, or none. That something is nonduality, which we will discuss next.

5

NONDUALITY

We distinguish between two types of ego-lessness, because that is how practitioners usually experience their path. At first, we discover an absence of self "inside," and later an absence of worldly reality "outside." For a time, those absences feel different, but with the insight of nonduality, we realize that they are one.

Nonduality is the condition of not being divided into two. In Buddha's Dharma, such a division never arises. If it does, our experience is not the true Dharma. A helpful metaphor for nonduality is the breaking of a vase. Originally, there seem to be two spaces, a space inside and outside of the vase. However, when the vase is broken, the spaces seem to merge, and are seen to be one, or none. This is akin to the experience of nonduality.

In my case, a year passed between my realizing egolessness of other and realizing nonduality.

During this year, I experienced a difference between egolessness of self, a space felt inside, and egolessness of other, which manifested mainly as the world having lost its reality. I never considered them as similar. Only in the moment of nonduality did they merge into one limitless space.

The experience occurred in my shrine room, when I happened to look at a small table near where I was sitting, and saw that its absence of reality felt exactly like the absence of self I had experienced for many years. It was an "aha" or "oh, that's how it is" moment, somewhat matter-of-fact, which is surprising considering the magnitude of the insight. This first nondual experience was of the unity of the two egolessnesses, and was limited to the coming together of those two originally disparate experiences.

Shortly afterwards, I walked into a supermarket, and looking at the neat, well-lit, brightly colored rows of fruits and vegetables, I observed nonduality more clearly, when I suddenly became everything I saw. There was no longer any split between what used to seem inside and the world outside. Inside was outside, and outside was inside. The *dualistic barrier*, which my teacher had described as that which separates self from other, had been removed like the Berlin Wall.

This was quite fortuitous, because when we experience two, they interact in sometimes painful ways, such as the *kleshas* (Sanskrit, "afflictions"): passion, aggression, ignorance, pride, and envy. Nonduality had removed that interaction, removing the friction between inside and outside.

This second experience of nonduality was much more vivid and profound than the first. Now, I did not merely realize the nonduality of the two egolessnesses, but the not-twoness of everything in the world and me.

Neither of these experiences of nonduality involved any stress, or any sense of letting go. Both resulted from continued meditation, just plugging along every day. Meditation is like that sometimes: after days or decades of practice, without a flourish, something happens. I remember hearing that Dilgo Khyentse Rinpoche once described his path as six months of practice and six months of receiving teachings each year, until after about forty years he got it. Buddhists do best starting early and living a long life, as was the case with him.

Like all major insights, realizing nonduality demands sustained effort, but it seems even then that non-duality is a particularly difficult part of the path. After around twenty years of engaging others in discussions about enlightenment, I find that they most frequently stumble on nonduality. They may either lack the preliminary insights that lead to nonduality, or, despite having them, find that it continues to elude them.

The non-Dharmic world runs on duality, and without seeing its alternative, few of us realize its presence. Our reality is split into a part inside us that stops at our skin (for some reason), and a separate world outside our skin—and this split seems so obvious that we never consider otherwise. For us to realize that we are actually an undivided space extending endlessly is asking a lot, but the Dharma asks a lot.

A persistent narrative in modern spirituality holds that all religions are one. Unity is commendable, but not at the expense of truth, and the reality is that theistic religions—those believing in an other of any description—are incompatible with Buddhism. Buddhism is nondualistic at its core, and this sets it apart from most other religions.

Of course, theists will say that at some point they become one with their other. Some even believe they are inherently that other. But God, or gods, will always remain better than their believers; no good theist will ever profess that they are as perfect as God. There will always be a difference between believer and believed, and dualism will persist.

To discover the unity of egolessness of self and egolessness of other is to realize nonduality. With this insight arises, simultaneously, what in my opinion is the single most important insight in Buddhism. It is known as emptiness, and it will be the subject of the next chapter.

6

EMPTINESS

Emptiness (or voidness, Sanskrit *shunyata*) is nothingness with a difference. Along with its inseparable companion, awareness, it is one of the two major aspects of enlightened mind and reality. Emptiness certainly has an element of nothingness; after all, it arises from the absence of self and of reality in the phenomenal world. However, the nothingness of emptiness also has qualities.

One quality of emptiness is its limitless spaciousness, which brings a sense of boundless freedom. That freedom is responsible for the bliss inherent in the experience. Emptiness also feels completely restful and peaceful, because it is what we truly are; no effort is required to be it. Since it transcends the constant interaction between self and other, emptiness also feels serene and free from conflict. It also feels full, with a pervading richness. As well, due to its peace, restfulness, and richness, emptiness brings a natural sense of kindness and caring for others, probably the most worthwhile of its qualities.

Emptiness is also unmoving. Being everywhere, it has no place to go, although thoughts and emotions do move through it like meteors in space. Over time, these activities in emptiness are also seen to be empty just like the space they move in, an insight that will become very important further down the path.

Lastly, the void is eternal. Being uncreated and impervious to destruction, it has always been and will always be, even if there are no humans to experience it. It is the true nature of reality, and as such will never change.

So how do we experience emptiness? First, we should know that it isn't easy. It is possible, though, with the mind's eye, also called the third eye. We can easily experience the mind's eye itself: it is what visualizes our childhood pet, or what we had for dinner last night. It's also what sees emptiness at the time of realization—or, more to the point, it is what sees itself.

The mind's eye apprehends emptiness directly, without concept or logic. As Chögyam Trungpa explains:

———————

At the peak of the shunyata experience, a real glimpse of shunyata, your logic wears out. You have no logic, no reference point of logic, and you become completely exposed to nothingness or fullness. [It is] a sudden glimpse of aloneness.

The Pocket Tibetan Buddhism Reader, 149.

———————

Note that the quote states that emptiness is full. This points to the truth that emptiness is a feeling, not something intellectually derived, and that a quality of that feeling is fullness or richness. Emptiness being *full* is one of a number of counterintuitive turns that typify emptiness, and realization in general.

I first saw emptiness, without a seer, when the experience of nonduality revealed that egolessness of self and egolessness of other were the same. At that moment, some twenty years ago, I felt a sudden wholeness, like a large part of me had been missing all my life. And it had: I had been dividing the world into this and that, and when they came together, I was finally complete.

At the same time, I also experienced the limitless nature of reality. Years before, I had sat in meditation with the great Nyingma master Dilgo Khyentse Rinpoche, and I heard him let out his breath over his microphone. Listening, I felt a start when the mind following his breath went somewhere rather scary—somewhere my own mind couldn't or wouldn't go.

With the insight of emptiness, I finally realized where Khyentse Rinpoche had gone.

The enlightened reality of emptiness is not of the physical world and physics, but of the world of mind's true nature. Emptiness does share with physics the property of being counterintuitive, however. Just as physics informs us that light is somehow both a wave and a particle, emptiness reveals other paradoxes. One, as mentioned, is that emptiness is full. Another is that emptiness is an experience without an experiencer, which doesn't make sense until we enter the realm of nonduality. As a topper, we also learn that emptiness is form, as described by one of the best-known Buddhist scriptures, the Heart Sutra:

Form is emptiness; emptiness also is form. Emptiness is no other than form; form is no other than emptiness. Thus, Shariputra, all dharmas are emptiness.

What does it mean that *form is emptiness*? For some time after first seeing emptiness, it may seem that form—cows, canyons, cathedrals—appear to be swimming in emptiness, immersed in it. This view led me for a time to feel that the sutra was imprecisely worded, or had been mistranslated through the millennia. Later, the truth dawned, and

I saw that form *is* emptiness, not floating in it, and the sutra was right all along. At this point, it became impossible to view form without also viewing emptiness, confirming that *all dharmas are emptiness*. Dharmas, as used in this sutra, are occurrences in the phenomenal world, and since form is emptiness, all dharmas share that quality. (As for Shariputra, he was a disciple of the Buddha known for his wisdom and teaching ability, and he asked the question that led to the Heart Sutra as an answer.)

So, form is truly emptiness, but what about the experience that *emptiness is form*? That's a bit trickier. We may think that since form is emptiness, seeing emptiness as form would naturally follow, but it doesn't. We can see how form is changed by emptiness; but we cannot see emptiness being changed into form. Emptiness is not a thing, so it is impossible to experience it as something becoming something else. What the sutra means is that if one conceptualizes or has any idea about emptiness, even so much as giving it that name, it immediately becomes form, something rather than nothing. Concept is what makes emptiness form.

The problem that concept poses to realizing emptiness cannot be overstated. The experience of emptiness is immediately dispelled by identifying with any ideas about its nature. As such, we should be very skeptical of any Buddhist who reports having realized emptiness through concept. That mistake is very old, dating back at least to a second-century CE Indian philosopher named Nagarjuna, who founded the Madhyamaka (Sanskrit, "Middle Way") school of Buddhism. Nagarjuna's writings on emptiness are compelling, until he gives his reason for asserting its existence:

We state that conditioned origination is emptiness. It is mere designation depending on something, and it is the middle path. Since nothing has arisen without depending on something, there is nothing that is not empty.

Mūlamadhyamakakārikā, 24.

What Nagarjuna did was take a teaching of the Buddha called "dependent origination," and use it as the basis for realizing emptiness. Dependent origination asserts that, since all things in the world are made of component parts—for example, a chair has legs, a back, and a seat—they are therefore empty of inherent existence. Being made of parts, they depend on those parts for their being, and hence have no being of their own.

This logic is perhaps somewhat helpful for an intellectual understanding of emptiness; but emptiness is an experience, and that experience cannot be arrived at by ratiocination, only by realization. Nagarjuna employed mundane *prajña*—logic—on a subject that required transcendent *prajña*, insight. With those lines, Nagarjuna established a conceptual understanding of emptiness that many Buddhists have confused with actual realization to this day.

Another obstacle to realizing shunyata consists of regarding it as a thing. It cannot be experienced by the senses, such as taste, touch, smell, sight, or hearing, so it is totally bereft of "thingness." Also, it cannot be found as a creation of mind, because it is mind itself. As such, it is hopeless to look for emptiness at any time, and especially during meditation. The urge is very great to see the void, but the more we try to see it, the further we drift from it, because filling our minds with seeking obscures what we wish to find.

The tendency to look for emptiness remains a problem even after we first experience the insight. Emptiness is very compelling—after all, it changes our entire perception of the world in a very pleasant way. As a result, we look for it. This is a silly thing to do, because once emptiness is first seen, it never leaves. Nevertheless, we do keep trying to see it, and in the process, we objectify it into something outside of ourselves. We then fruitlessly pursue this objectified concept.

This habit may persist for some time. In my case, after first having the insight, I was still beset with wanting—wanting's power is amazing—and so I relapsed into trying to recreate what I had already experienced. This held me back for some time, until I realized that I *was* emptiness, and that there was no longer any need to search for it.

We can also struggle to experience the void due to a lack of mindfulness, when our attachment to thoughts and emotions clouds the experience. Mindfulness is often presented as an early part of the Buddhist path, but it remains crucial through the highest levels of insight. All levels of practitioners have thoughts and emotions that carry us away from the now, the only place where insight can be appreciated, and only mindfulness can return us to it.

As of this writing, the benefits of emptiness are still unfolding in my life. As a recent example, I find that I am now relying less on seeing form as emptiness as a means to experience emptiness itself. As such, I am less "drawn out" by that realization: although form is still emptiness, it now serves more to remind me of the emptiness I am, rather than of the emptiness inherent in form. The result is that I feel the stability of emptiness more, especially in interacting with other people. I used to abandon emptiness in my commitment to others, while now, being more settled in emptiness and mind, I remain in emptiness, see them more clearly, and understand them better. I find that I can be of more benefit to them, often just by listening and seeing what is important to them. I attribute my progress on the insight of emptiness in large part to various meditation practices, and to the guru and his lineage that those practices invoke.

To summarize, emptiness is a many-splendored nothing, and the basis of reality. It can change the world into an Eden with its presence, and it is eternal. What more could one ask? Yet, a question remains. How can we know all these things about emptiness? That brings us to our next topic: awareness.

7

AWARENESS

Awareness is what allows us to experience events, to perceive ourselves and the world. Buddhism includes this commonsense understanding of awareness, and goes further. It reveals not only what awareness does, but what it *is*.

A major advantage of awareness relative to most Buddhist insights is the ease of experiencing it—as we would expect from something that continually makes the world knowable to us. Unlike, say, emptiness, which usually requires years of effort to experience, awareness is always present and accessible. The challenge is not in encountering it, but in knowing what we have encountered. As usual with Buddhist insights, true or enlightened awareness has numerous counterintuitive qualities. For example, although awareness undoubtedly exists, it does not exist as a thing, so it is not something we can measure or weigh, or buy a pint of. Moreover, it abides self-existingly, meaning it is not created by us or anyone else. In other words, it has never been created, and therefore can never be destroyed.

A mirror is a helpful metaphor for some of awareness's qualities. Like a mirror, self-existing awareness is always there, yet it makes no effort to be aware; it does so naturally, like a mirror reflecting an image. Also, like a mirror, awareness has no bias, so it does not differentiate one thing from another. Orchids or offal are all the same to it, because it has no concepts about what appears in it.

This sameness of appearances is known as their quality of *Thatness* or *Suchness*. When we first look at an object, it is always That before we categorize it. With awakened awareness, however, objects are never categorized, and remain as That. Our body becomes the same as a chair in the Thatness of awakened awareness. On the other hand, awareness can still discern the difference between a tree and a cell tower (although that has become a bit trickier of late).

Awareness is also like a mirror in that what the mirror reflects *is* the mirror. There is no separation between a mirror and the images appearing in it; and so it is with awareness, as the famous Nyingma teacher Tulku Urgyen Rinpoche explains:

The perceived, the experiential contents that are usually called "appearances" are in actuality never separate from empty cognizance [awareness].

Rainbow Painting, 168.

We are what we see; no duality arises between the seer and seen. This is true not only of sight, but of all our senses. For some, it is most evident with cricket sounds. In China and Japan, people keep crickets as pets because of their chirp's immediacy to the mind. Something about that sound on a still summer night reveals the truth that sound and what hears it are the same.

Overall, we can summarize awareness with some lines from a Dzogchen Buddhist tantra (Dzogchen being the highest level of Vajrayana Buddhism, and particularly attuned to the enlightened aspects of awareness):

Amazing, natural awareness is beyond thought.

Vividly clear, there is no obscuration.

Nakedly manifest, there is no delusion.

Wide awake, there is no subject or object.

As It Is, 209.

These lines reaffirm that awareness is nondualistic ("no subject or object"), naturally existing ("natural awareness"), not the result of any agency, especially concept ("beyond thought"), and that its inherent nature is not obscured or confused ("no obscuration, no delusion").

While we can enjoy such vivid and pithy descriptions intellectually, actually realizing them, as with most insights, presents difficulties. As is true of emptiness, concept is anathema to awareness. In almost the very instant in which we perceive an object, we label it as something, sometimes inappropriately. I remember once, at the beginning of a group meditation retreat, being convinced that a fellow retreatant disliked me. After sitting for a while and getting to know him, I realized that I had completely fabricated his dislike—in fact, when I asked him, he said he hadn't noticed me. This is a small demonstration of how concept warps awareness.

Moreover, with everyday awareness, experience is split into someone inside of us being aware of something outside. Physics speaks of the importance of the "observer effect" in distorting the nature of the phenomenon being observed. Splitting awareness into something inside observing something outside has much the same effect, because what is "inside" generates biases about what is "outside"—therefore changing how we perceive it.

Because of these difficulties, practitioners sometimes spend decades in retreat studying awareness. In my own case, I believe that if I had meditated solely on awareness, I would never have realized its nature—which is emptiness. Only by realizing emptiness first did I subsequently see the empty nature of awareness.

Similarly, in the process of experiencing emptiness, I also realized the not-two-ness of myself and objects, but I failed to apply that insight to the inseparability of objects and perception. Only after spending some time discussing the Dharma with Dzogchen practitioners, who use awareness as their key to enlightenment and are well-versed in it, did I overcome that obstacle. Hearing them describe objects and what observed them as inseparable prompted me to examine this claim experientially, and in a short time I saw it to be true. Experiencing that I *was* objects and that they were me was very close to realizing that I was also what I perceived, so it required only a small intuitive jump.

With regard to the problem of realizing awareness as self-existing (without an owner), I'm not sure when that insight arose. Of course, by its nature emptiness cannot have an owner, so I knew that about emptiness, and I surmise that that's how I came to realize awareness is self-existing. Whatever the case, since that insight, awareness has always seemed like something coming to me or being me, rather than being my creation. This aspect of its nature is also how I know that mind will continue after the body dies.

I'm similarly unsure when I realized that enlightened awareness does not label objects, but perceives them as the same in Thatness or Suchness. My sense is that, as with my experience of seeing awareness as nondual, this came simply from taking a closer look at the nature of awareness. Coming as I did from the Mahamudra tradition, which highlights the emptiness aspect of enlightened mind, I was less experienced in the awareness aspect emphasized in Dzogchen. When I devoted more time to awareness, my experience of it became more refined.

This stepwise description of my progress in understanding awareness applies to the Dharma in general. As in science, new discoveries generally spring from previous ones, and this is why never giving up in the Dharma is so important.

When we realize both emptiness and self-existing awareness, we have realized the two essential components of enlightened mind. At this point, we are considered "realized," or, in some traditions, as on the "path of seeing" or as having the "view." This is a major milestone, wherein reality transforms from a claustrophobic, egocentric, obstacle-ridden, dualistic, poorly observed, limited world to a limitless, non-centralized, restful, peaceful, vividly apparent, eternal one.

Even at this stage, we still have a long way to go on the path to enlightenment. Much more effort is required, particularly in meditation, as Lodro Thaye reminds us:

The one who does not meditate, but merely holds the view

Is like a rich man tethered by stinginess.

He is unable to bring appropriate fruition to himself and others.

Joining the view and meditation is the holy tradition.

The Rain of Wisdom, 84.

With the attainment of the view, we enter a new world governed by absolute truth, rather than by the relative truth we have always known. Our path now becomes learning how to accommodate the still-present confused or relative world into the enlightened or absolute one for the benefit of others. In the next chapter, we will see how that is done.

8

CONFUSION DAWNING AS WISDOM

At this point on the path, we have had the extraordinary good fortune, through the teacher, teachings, practices, sangha, and life experiences, to realize that we are emptiness inseparable from awareness, the true nature of mind. Even so, we still live in the relative or confused world, and we must deal with its dualism—"me and mine," "this and that," and the unpleasant results of their interactions. Although we know of another, more congenial world, the confused one still remains.

It is time to take another step on the path, and learn to integrate the chaotic world into the enlightened one for the benefit of ourselves and others. As the 11th-century Kagyu lineage holder Gampopa states in the last of his Four Dharmas, we must create a situation where "confusion dawns as wisdom." We now have the tools to do that, but we have not yet learned how to use them.

In life, everyone wishes to transform confusion into wisdom, but most of us are unsuccessful. The world is always churning up situations like sickness, money problems, and relationship breakups, which generate anguish, confusion, and unhappiness for us. Few of us know what to do with these experiences when they arise. Drugs, entertainment, and belief systems offer only temporary fixes, and they end up creating more problems than they solve.

As Dharma practitioners, we learn to recognize the occurrences of mind, and to work with them by refraining from accepting or rejecting them. Without the insight of emptiness, however, these techniques only soften mind's occurrences without removing them. They linger, buzzing around like flies that we can shoo, but never banish.

Fortunately, the space of mind expands and mind's energies shrink as we progress on the path, so the energies create less disturbance when they arise. I remember Chögyam Trungpa Rinpoche describing thoughts as being like "ripples on a pond." I also remember thinking that a lot depends on how big the pond is. He had a very big pond—a mind without limit—so thoughts that occurred in it only generated little ripples. At the time, I had a mud puddle, which sloshed over at the slightest agitation. I didn't know then that to get only ripples requires a pond as big as emptiness.

I worked as a physician with a lot of stress each day, caring for the sick and trying to have a worthwhile private life. To ease my burden, I read extensively in self-help, philosophy, and Western medicine, until I eventually found Buddhism and what for me was the best approach to the relative world. In my case, I needed to learn how to face energy and deal with it, rather than allowing it to unnerve me. I began in Zen and it helped, but I didn't really start working with the world's confusing energies until I became a practitioner of Vajrayana Buddhism. At that point, I saw that it was designed especially to transmute confusion into wisdom.

Of course, all Buddhist traditions help with this process, but it is the specialty of the Vajrayana. When we look at the vivid colors of Vajrayana robes and shrine rooms, and hear its loud piercing music and its drumming chants, we understand that energy—and incorporating it into mind—plays a large role in what the Vajrayana does.

Because of its promise of help with confusion, I entered the Vajrayana believing that it was suited for me, not realizing what it would require of me—or that I was in fact jumping from the frying pan into the fire. In particular, I didn't know what a problem ego would be in the process of transforming confusion into wisdom. Painfully and over a long time, I discovered that if ego rather than emptiness attempts to work with confusion, the energy of confusion fries ego, and its possessor.

As we progress in the Dharma, because of the practices, we begin to open; and as a result, we encounter *more* energy rather than less. For a long time, my Buddhist practice was heightening my stress rather than alleviating it, but I was so desperate for relief that I expected the next practice or program to save me. If I'd known what I was getting into, I wouldn't have done it, and I would have also missed the chance to transmute confusion into wisdom.

The pivotal event in my Vajrayana journey was the experience of emptiness. That is what really helped me to deal with my life and to help others. Emptiness is the complete resolution to the problem of *duhkha*, the stress of life: it alone provides permanent relief, free of any unpleasant side effects.

When we *become* emptiness, at least in my case, we soon observe that thoughts and emotions are also empty. How fortuitous, because we now have the shared emptiness of the occurrences of mind, and of mind itself, in which to dissolve those occurrences.

And they merge quite smoothly, like waves in the ocean, with emptiness being the water that makes up both the waves and the ocean. At this point, we are able to integrate what arises in mind—and all experiences do—into the absolute world in which they arise. This is how we can transmute the chaos of the relative world into the tranquility of the absolute.

"Practice makes perfect" applies here. Again and again, both in meditation and everyday life, we observe the activities of mind, and how they merge into its empty aware nature, until the process becomes a reflex. This is not a mechanical process where we try to convert one thing into another, but a merging that happens very quickly, naturally, and without effort, as long as we remain in the empty, aware nature of mind. The trick lies in remaining in that nature, and allowing its awareness both to see occurrences arise, and to see that those occurrences are not different in emptiness from the mind they arise in. As Shunryu Suzuki Roshi teaches:

People who know the state of emptiness will always be able to dissolve their problems by constancy.

Zen Mind, Beginner's Mind, 83.

By "constancy," Suzuki Roshi means remaining in a state of emptiness. Although this process occurs naturally and effortlessly, it may not be consistent, because thoughts and emotions tend to obscure mind's true nature. In my experience, emotions, with their heightened energy, are easier for mind to see and dissolve, while thoughts, which carry less energy, are sneakier and more apt to develop into trains of thought that obscure enlightened mind.

Mastery comes with continued application. Through meditation, we learn to remain in enlightened mind longer, see mental impulses better, and not get carried away by them. No longer falling prey to thoughts and emotions benefits both us and those we share our lives with, who begin to trust our sanity, and to relax and open to us.

To this point, we have described the liberation of confusion by emptiness. In order for confusion to dawn as *wisdom*, we have to take another step on the path.

In the Dharma, wisdom is not something we apply. It is the open, aware nature of mind. At first, we act like we have that mind, by taking a neutral stance toward mental occurrences—emulating what enlightened mind does naturally. Later, when we experience that the nature of mind is emptiness inseparable from awareness, we see how the empty occurrences of mind are naturally one with it in emptiness. There is a further stage of wisdom as well. After practitioners pacify the occurrences of mind, wisdom takes on a new dimension: instead of only pacifying the energies of emotions, it uses them to benefit others.

This new form of wisdom requires some new Buddhist terms. The first is Buddha nature (Sanskrit *tathagatagarbha*). Buddha nature is the truth that, however confused we may be, our innate nature is always enlightened. Buddha nature, when developed, is like a prism that refracts light—or in Buddhism, energy. That energy expresses itself in five basic ways known as the Buddha Families. Chögyam Trungpa Rinpoche describes these families and their energies:

The buddha family or families associated with a person describe his or her fundamental style, that person's intrinsic perspective or stance in perceiving the world and working with it. Each family is associated with both a neurotic and an enlightened style. The neurotic expression of any buddha family can be transmuted into its wisdom or enlightened aspect.

Secrets of the Vajra World, 131.

People of the *vajra* (Sanskrit, "diamond") family are analytical, with a strong neurotic tendency toward anger and irritation. Transmuted into enlightened wisdom, their energy is clarity, acute judgment, and ability to suss out the inaccuracies or falsities of any situation. *Ratna* ("jewel") people tend to overextend themselves beyond sensible limits, and to develop excessive pride. Transmuted, their energy enriches the world, making it more welcoming and pleasant for themselves and others. *Padma* ("lotus") people are consumed with neurotic wanting, acquisition, and seduction. Their enlightened energy is a strong awareness of and appreciation for the different qualities of any situation. *Karma* ("action") people are neurotically competitive, wanting to outdo and dominate others. Their enlightened energy is to smoothly, efficiently accomplish whatever is required. Finally, there is the *buddha* ("authentic one") family, whose neurosis is to neglect the world. As a glass rolls off a table, the buddha style is to say, "That glass may roll off the table," without doing anything to stop it. Their enlightened quality is spaciousness, an ability to calmly accommodate stressful and demanding energies.

Most people have one or two prominent styles or energies, but we all have the potential for each of the others, and as a result we possess all the energies needed for complete wisdom. When we tap into the enlightened wisdom of the Buddha families, confusion then truly dawns as wisdom. For example, if someone becomes competitive with a person with karma wisdom, that person uses the competitive energy in a wise way to easily accomplish a task. A person with vajra wisdom, aggressively confronted over an issue, will trenchantly expose the flaws in the issue. If an individual becomes obsessed about an unaccomplished goal, someone with padma wisdom may suggest another, equally rewarding possibility that better suits that person.

When someone transmutes confusion into wisdom in this way, everything he or she does points out how to approach life correctly. To average people, on the other hand, these people may appear difficult, because "nothing works on them." Insults, praise, and temptations have no impact on them, quite unlike regular people, and energies aimed at them rebound in unexpected and sometimes painfully revealing ways. I am reminded of a hirsute lady I knew, who once provocatively asked Chögyam Trungpa Rinpoche why he had a suit on. He replied, "Why do you have a mustache?"

Up to this point, we have emphasized insight and wisdom. We have seen how wisdom progresses on the path, and how confusion dawning as wisdom benefits both ourselves and others. Along with wisdom,

Dharma has another aspect, and a very important one. It is said that the bird of enlightenment flies on two wings, wisdom and compassion. We will look at the wing of compassion next, and learn how to fly to the aid of others.

9

COMPASSION

Like all insights in Buddhism, compassion (Sanskrit *karuna*) is felt. The feeling of compassion brings a natural sense of richness that expands limitlessly. Accompanying that richness is an unconditional confidence, one that is not confident about anything in particular, but simply abides in confidence.

This state of compassion is unafraid to extend itself for the benefit of others. It appreciates others, feels their suffering, and cares about them without contrivance. When the compassionate mind sees another human, it feels a natural attraction to that person, like a plant turning toward the sun. Also, in advanced insight the question of worthiness never arises, so mind makes no distinctions about who it helps, much like good physicians aid anyone who requires their care.

In conjunction with compassion, wisdom plays a valuable role. Wisdom sees situations clearly, so it does not allow others to be smothered with too much care, or frozen without it. Together with compassion, wisdom provides the perfect complement for benefiting others.

We should not mistake authentic compassion for its counterfeits. Compassion without wisdom, for example, has been called "idiot compassion," and the unexamined charity this phrase points to is quite prevalent in modern society. I remember a food fund that was soliciting donations at a table outside a food market I use. I paused in front of the table and shared with the lady that I didn't trust charities. She said that I could simply give food rather than money, but not wanting to do the extra work, I donated money. Lo and behold, that same year the local news reported that the CEO of the food fund had stolen money from it. That was the last straw for me. Now, If I give to the needy, I donate food or goods, not money. I've been burned enough by idiot compassion.

Moreover, compassion is not a function of the amount of money given, or of any other such external metric, but of the purity of the giver's intent. Egoless compassion is better than money, if it acknowledges the worth of others, smiles, says hello, and asks them how they are feeling. Caring in small, everyday ways is as good as gold.

Lastly, authentic compassion never has an agenda. Any whiff of ego-serving blights the benefits compassion provides. This is one reason why emptiness is so important. Only the total spaciousness of emptiness, without its concern for self and other, can lead to unsullied caring.

We all feel compassion from time to time, but for it to become wholly what we are, we will have to progress through a number of stages. The first inkling of caring emerges in meditation, where by calmly observing mind, we begin to develop a relationship with it. Gradually, we understand negativity to be just another occurrence in mind, rather than something that harshly defines who we are, and we relax more and become less rigid toward ourselves.

As we relax further, and begin to accept what occurs in mind, we find that its upheavals become more workable, and we begin to develop a relationship with it that naturally evolves into kindness toward ourselves. This is the beginning of compassion, and by our unconditionally accepting who or what we are, it begins to emerge.

As we continue to lose our fixed attitudes toward ourselves, we may even discover that the holder of those attitudes has disappeared. Then we discover the kindest thing we can do for ourself: see that we don't have one.

Making friends with one's self—and, especially, seeing that it doesn't exist—frees us to turn to the needs of others. Not until the experience of emptiness, however, can we do so completely. With emptiness, our heart, along with all else, becomes empty and free of attachments. As Reginald Ray says in his excellent book, *Secrets of the Vajra World*:

This empty heart has nothing to say for itself, nothing to assert, nothing even to hope for or—as the *Heart Sutra* says—to fear. However, such an empty heart is one that is ever available to others. It is one without an agenda, but with a ready tenderness and responsiveness to another person's suffering and confusion. A realization of emptiness, then, is the precondition for genuine compassion. And such an empty heart, though desolate from ego's standpoint, is an expression of the wisdom that sees the utter and unbreachable freedom of our essential being.

Secrets of the Vajra World, 96.

And so, with emptiness and an empty heart, the conditions are established for complete compassion. Empty heart has no bias, so it is not influenced by circumstances; as such, it remains open and responsive to the needs of others. Furthermore, emptiness in general is endowed with complete freedom, and those who enjoy that freedom and the joy that arises from it naturally wish to share their good fortune with others. As an example, the sole reason why Buddhas devote themselves to others is to help them attain enlightenment and realize its benefits. The enlightened mind of a Buddha contains such immeasurable freedom and richness that simply being it fulfills all their needs, and they would never leave it except for their commitment to share it with others.

As mentioned previously, compassion is, along with wisdom, one of the two wings of the bird of enlightenment. These two wings are what we truly are when enlightened mind transcends its obscurations. With both compassion and wisdom, the bird of enlightenment has the wings it needs to fly, as the Kagyu master Khenpo Tsultrim Gyamtso Rinpoche explains:

When the unsound state consisting in the deluded state of mind has been eliminated, in other words, when the knowledge which realizes nonself has been brought to final perfection, this is buddhahood. Or we could look at it from the other angle, when great compassion imbued with loving kindness has been brought to final perfection, the name "buddha" is used to describe the person who has accomplished this.

The result is that through the power inherent in compassion one works for the benefit of beings and through the power inherent in finally perfected knowledge one comprehends fully and in their infinite variety the ways of benefiting beings in individual cases.

Indestructible Truth, 443.

In this egoless setting, caring manifests in surprising ways. My son and I, on separate occasions, received teachings from the same Vajrayana guru. As a result of his blessings, we both then walked out of his talk and stopped to interact with strangers—myself a homeless person, himself a woman with a physical deformity—something neither of us does normally. The teacher's compassion had transferred itself to us, revealing where we had to go next on the path to enlightenment.

Sometimes, compassion takes the form of a reprimand. This is unpleasant for the recipient, but truly compassionate people will employ censure when necessary. I remember one occasion when my teacher visited the meditation center where I lived. I had recently broken up with a girlfriend, and I was not talking to her. As my teacher walked down our greeting line, where my ex-girlfriend stood next to me with perhaps a dozen people in line on either side, he shook hands with everyone before me and everyone after me, but not me. The reprimand was clear: "Do you see what it feels like when someone ignores you?" He could not possibly have known of my situation with my girlfriend, as he had just arrived by plane. What he did was spontaneous, just another indication of his magic.

A proviso is in order about compassion with an edge: we must be careful not to fall into justifying our own harsh behavior as compassionate. "Tough love" is sometimes trotted out in Buddhist circles, but I always have reservations about it. I suspect a lot of aggression is inflicted on students by teachers in the guise of "tough love." In any case, corrective compassion must only be employed by realized beings. For all others, kindness should be the order of the day. And if it becomes impossible to avoid correcting another, we should do so with the knowledge that a sharp knife needs but a small amount of pressure to cut.

My own experience of compassion has developed over the years, in concert with specific events in my life. Over time, I have become more awake and less caught up in my mental feed, and as I see more clearly, I begin to penetrate the implications of situations.

Noticing two people sitting humbly at a lunch counter pierces my heart—not because of something they do, but because of their unadorned humanity.

Also, as I progress on the path, I become bigger—limitless, in fact—and caring about another no longer feels like it requires a piece of me that I can't afford. I have become wealthy enough, just existing, to share my benefits with others. None of this evolves intellectually but as a felt experience accompanying greater insight.

I have become a warmer person generally, but sometimes compassion comes to me in flashes that generate an impetus to do something. A small, crippled man walking along the highway prompts an immediate pull-over to give him a ride. Although my experience of compassion is growing through the years, I feel the process will never end, and that I will never be compassionate enough. Nevertheless, I persist, and I am pleased with any signs of progress.

Even the early steps of caring are a boon to ourselves and others. Those of us who don't like ourselves—burdened by our looks, lack of education, lack of love, money needs, prior traumas, or countless other problems—struggle with our pain, and so have little time for others. As a former physician, I know the time pressure involved in caring for others, and how easily we can slight people who would like to share more of their lives with us. Sometimes, just a few more minutes away from our own needs and some attentive listening can mean a great deal to others.

More developed compassion is the fast path to nonduality, because it entails no division between the one who experiences compassion and the objects of it. What was once another's problem becomes ours as well. I saw this sensitivity develop in me as a physician on the Buddhist path. Initially, I felt my purpose was to diagnose a patient's problem and treat him or her appropriately. This was true, but as I progressed in both Buddhism and medicine, I realized there was much more to provide. I began to open more to my patients, and understand more of the nuances of what they felt. They immediately sensed that they were now people to me—not just diagnoses—and that I cared about them. What they felt then was often as helpful as what I prescribed.

Of the countless approaches that have been devised to make our lives better, compassion is one that actually works. When it is unconditional, it can change the world. If it were universal, problems like crime and destitution would cease to exist, and humanity would truly become one. Sadly, though, we often find compassion missing where it should be most abundant, such as in our religions. Despite having the examples of Jesus and Buddha, we practice religion uncompassionately, to the point of killing others because of their beliefs. However, with a true understanding of the nature of reality, along with caring, the bird of enlightenment can fly to all spiritual traditions and peoples of our planet, bringing them the loving kindness and compassion they so badly need.

10

MAGIC

Magic (Sanskrit *siddhi*, meaning "fulfillment" or "accomplishment"), is a lesser-known part of the path to enlightenment. Siddhi has both a relative and an absolute aspect. Of the two, absolute siddhi is superior, and refers simply to the attainment of enlightenment. Lesser or relative siddhi, the subject of this chapter, is the ability to influence the everyday world in magical ways.

Relative siddhi emerges from working with energy. Energy is a natural part of human existence—it is what we feel with emotions like a hot burst of anger or a throb of fear. If we learn how to work with these energies, and then engage the regular world with them, siddhis appear.

I saw this on a number of occasions with my teacher Chögyam Trungpa Rinpoche, an enlightened being who was totally without fear and who engaged fully with the world's energies. I once approached him and said, "It's nice to see you, Sir"—and he disappeared before my eyes, demonstrating his humorous as well as magical touch. The Zen master Shunryu Suzuki Roshi performed a similar feat with one of his Western students:

While Suzuki looked down at the creek, Ken saw him disappear, blending totally with the water, wood, and air. A moment later they were walking down the dirt and cobble path and toward the zendo. Ken didn't know what had happened, or if it had happened to him, to Suzuki, or both.

Crooked Cucumber, 339.

On another occasion, my teacher read my mind, and shocked me for several minutes with something he intuited about me. The matter is still so sensitive that I am unable to recount it some forty years later. Others reported similar experiences, and, in general, it was well-known in the sangha that he could read minds. In fact, in one talk he said, "I know your deepest secrets"—and he did.

At another talk, on the importance of mindful speech, he mentioned that if we spoke correctly, we could prevent a traffic ticket. The next day, outside the site of the previous day's talk, I took a wrong turn up a one-way street, and a policeman pulled me over. The police in that town took no prisoners, so I knew I was in trouble, but remembering what my teacher had said, I spoke as precisely and grammatically as possible. The policeman let me off. Rinpoche had not only predicted my future, but had demonstrated to me personally the importance of mindful speech.

I could relate many more experiences of Rinpoche's magic, but I will mention a special one that occurred at Shambhala Mountain Center, a spiritually empowered place he founded. In the years after his death, I visited there often, since it was near my home in Colorado. On one visit, sitting in meditation in one of the shrine rooms, I happened to look over to his teaching chair, and found him sitting in it. As I watched, he lifted a glass of sake to his lips. At that same moment, one of the shrine candles overflowed, making a gurgling noise so loud that others commented on it later. Rinpoche then put down his drink, turned to me, and smiled.

Relative siddhis are not aberrations that just pop up now and then, but are an actual element of Buddhist lineages throughout millennia. A well-known example in Vajrayana Buddhism are the 84 *mahasiddhas* (Sanskrit, "those with great magic"), who lived from 750 to 1150 CE on the Indian subcontinent. The mahasiddhas were people who held various occupations, from king to pimp, and through their siddhis brought others to enlightenment. Many were social outcasts, who lived in the charnel grounds where dead bodies were deposited. Because some of the vagrants in India were not cremated, their bodies were left in charnel grounds to decompose. The mahasiddhas lived in these charnel grounds for both practical and religious purposes: no one bothered them there, and since the grounds were terrifying—not only from the bodies strewn about, but from the malignant spirits that inhabited them—they created powerful energies that the siddhas sought.

One of the great mahasiddhas was Tilopa, an Indian who lived in the 11th century and worked as a pimp at night and a pounder of sesame seeds during the day. As the story goes:

One day, as predicted, his accomplishment came to its perfection. One and all then saw him seated in space in the heart of a tent of rainbow lights, at a height of about seven coconut trees above ground level.

Tilopa, 16.

Not only was Tilopa magical, but his influence continues to this day in the practices and teachings of Vajrayana Buddhism. His insights are recorded, and the nature of his mind has been passed down through the centuries, including to my teacher and his students.

As with many of the occurrences in Buddhism, siddhis cannot be sought. Any attempt to manufacture them will preclude them entirely. Certain practices may arouse siddhis, but their actual appearance is unpredictable and spontaneous. In my experience, relative siddhis mean little to those who have them—which is one reason why they have them. In their case, relative siddhis are simply epiphenomena of the much more important absolute siddhi of enlightenment.

A connection to the teacher and lineage is crucial to relative siddhi, because the siddhis arise from devotion to one's teacher, who then transmits the blessings—the high-octane feelings—emanating from the lineage. Those blessings become the source of siddhi. As such, when we experience magic, it's quite clear that it comes from the teacher. We may or may not be directly in the teacher's presence when it occurs, but it's clear that he or she is making it happen.

Lastly, we ourselves have a role to play. If we don't believe in magic—and I tend not to, except when I witness it with my teacher—we won't recognize it. So, there has to be magic, and *we* have to be open to it.

How do teachers manifest siddhis? I don't know. My unsupported feeling about relative siddhi is that it is a creation of the universal unconscious. (When someone uses impressive but nebulous words like "universal unconscious" to explain something, we can be sure they are in over their head. And I am.) Having experienced magic many times, it seems to me that the magicians are hooked into a level of mind beyond our ken. They experience things that are hidden from us until they awaken us to them, like events in the future or our innermost thoughts. Again, though, the real truth is that I don't know how siddhis happen. If I did, they wouldn't be siddhis.

To mention magic in Buddhism has possible draw-backs. People are susceptible to fascination with woo-woo experiences, and some spiritual entrepreneurs use this fascination to sell Vajrayana magic and lead students on fruitless spiritual trips. Nevertheless, magic *is* part of the Buddhist path, at least in some traditions, and mentioning it is appropriate. For those of us who wish to be magical ourselves, I recommend that we first experience the magic of emptiness—without an experiencer—and then see what happens.

In this and the preceding chapters, we have seen the nature of some of the insights that arise on the path to enlightenment. In the next chapters, we will examine the characteristics of that path, and the supports required to travel it.

SUPPORTS ON THE PATH

11

WHAT THE PATH IS

Like any journey, the Buddhist path entails both pleasant and difficult conditions. Unquestionably, the path is challenging throughout, even for longtime practitioners, but beginners seem to struggle the most. Like an inexperienced hiker's blisters and sore muscles, untrained minds carry their own forms of discomfort, including burning boredom, chilling doubt, and unremitting deluges of thoughts and emotions, to name a few. Along with these obstacles, practitioners also encounter unexpected boosts in insight to help them, like a refreshing pond or beautiful bird song on a regular path.

As with a physical path, the Buddhist path has sidetracks, and we must quickly notice them, or we risk undoing years or even lifetimes of effort. One common error is simply quitting, often because the commitment seems too great and we feel that we're not getting anywhere. We may also fall prey to various kinds of ideas—our own or others'—that drag us off the authentic path into miasmas of mistaken concepts. And, of course, simply living presents endless obstacles: physical or mental illnesses that cloud the mind with pain and fear, work and family demands that fill our minds with stress and rob us of time for spiritual practices, and the always-present specter of death.

We are not alone, however, in navigating these challenges on the Buddhist path. We will encounter numerous fellow travelers, all with their own questions, convictions, and tendencies. They will share with us the camaraderie of confusion, specifically about who they are and the true nature of reality, and they will all have egos, which will have played a big role in their entering the path.

Travelers begin on the path for varied reasons, from feeling something click on seeing a Buddha statue, to being drawn in by a book title, to seeking relief for intense psychological pain. Past masters have had similar, diverse motivations. Milarepa, an 11th-century Tibetan Buddhist saint, was driven by guilt for killing others with magic (one of his nicknames was "the Great Magician"). Naropa, an 11th-century Indian Buddhist scholar, realized he didn't really know what the words he was teaching meant. Bankei, a 17th-century Japanese Zen master, wanted to know at all costs what enlightenment was:

———

One day, the class was taking up the Great Learning, one of the "four books" of Confucianism. The teacher came to the central words, "'The way of great learning lies in clarifying bright virtue." Bankei interrupted the teacher. "What is bright virtue?" he asked. The teacher, repeating the glosses given in one of the traditional commentaries, answered, "The intrinsic nature of good in each person." Bankei asked what the intrinsic nature of man was and was told, "It's his fundamental nature." "Then what is that?" he persisted. "The ultimate truth of heaven," replied the teacher. None of these answers satisfied Bankei. A deeper explanation was needed.

Unborn, 5.

———

Even as a youth, Bankei had a dogged desire for truth, and this exemplifies the attitude of many successful travelers on the path. In Bankei's case, it took him to Buddhism, and enlightenment.

Buddhists take various approaches to the path. For example, Zen Buddhists may use koans or sayings to exhaust their rational minds, or Vajrayana Buddhists may engage in visualization practices to discover their own true nature. In rare cases, a Buddhist practitioner may travel the whole path in one instant—as the 6th Zen Patriarch, Huineng, was said to have done after hearing his teacher recite a single line from a Buddhist treatise called the *Diamond Sutra*. The line reads, "One should activate one's mind so it has no attachment," and it points to the giving up necessary for complete insight to occur.

Whatever approach we take, there is only one Buddhist path: the path to enlightenment. This is true even for Buddhists who report having no interest in enlightenment. Since we're all on the same path, it behooves us to be properly outfitted for it; just as hikers need equipment (good clothing, footwear, backpack, and a map), practitioners need specific supports on the journey.

12

THE TEACHER

Like shoes and clothing on a regular path, the path to enlightenment requires certain indispensable supports. The first is a teacher, in the flesh.

Many people maintain that a living teacher is not necessary on the Buddhist path, and that practitioners who depend on one are needy, feckless, and insecure—weaknesses that the teacher will exploit for his or her benefit. This belief has gained momentum as more exposés of teachers sexually molesting their students come to light. Furthermore, technology has replaced much of what living mentors used to provide. We can now hear and see instructors on the internet, and easily access Buddhist teachings and meditation techniques.

A problem with following absentee teachers, however, is ego. Without the help of a personal mentor who has walked the path and seen ego's subtleties, we will invariably stray. Caught by our ideas of where the path leads, and without the help of an experienced guide, we will wander into conceptual wastelands, without knowing we are lost.

Moreover, no book or video is nearly as instructive as actually seeing a realized master carry on his or her life: relating with others, dealing with disappointments, and mindfully performing the smallest tasks. For these reasons and many others, a personal teacher of the Dharma (Buddhist truth and experience) is indispensable.

Different Dharma teachers fill different roles. Some relay their knowledge of the Dharma; others, through their conduct, exemplify its moral precepts; and a few actually embody the fruition of the path and transmit it to others.

Authentic teachers will also assume different roles at different stages on the student's path. In Vajrayana Buddhism, as one example, teachers begin as elders who introduce students to the Buddhist teachings, behavioral guidelines, and meditation. Later, they become a spiritual friend (*kalyanamitra*). Through teaching and example, they show students how to benefit others, thereby revealing the essence of Buddhism. Finally, they manifest as the guru, and through various skillful means—some psychologically painful to the student—point out the true nature of reality.

Discussing teachers raises an immediate question: how can we find the right one? Predictably, opinions vary. One school of thought holds that we don't need to search for a teacher, because the right one will appear when we are ready. Leaving something so important to karma may not be the best approach, however, particularly with the brevity of life.

So we need to be proactive. However, thinking about finding a Dharma teacher in this day and age brings to mind the phrase *caveat emptor*: let the buyer beware. Buddhism's introduction to the West has brought with it a spate of sexual misconduct by mentors in the Dharma. A Dharma teacher, especially with a title and robes, can easily lure naïve students, or social climbers, into liaisons they regret. Teachers may also steal, and buy mansions and fleets of cars with the funds of their true believers.

Another problem—which may seem minor but is not—are those who do not know the meaning of the words they teach. Without actual experience, they pervert the teachings, and students unable to discern authentic from inauthentic become guileless victims. This issue exists even at the highest levels of spirituality. Words are already misleading as guideposts to truth in the Dharma, and adding a confused instructor creates an even greater barrier for those trying to progress on the path to enlightenment.

Writing in *The Lion's Roar*, Lewis Richmond outlines five ways to approach searching for a teacher:

1) Watch: Observe what the teacher says and does. Note how he or she treats people. Is the teacher kind, friendly, and humble? Does the teacher have a sense of humor, and is he or she forthright and honest?

2) Ask Questions: Ask the teacher about any issues you may have, and, especially ask existing students if there are any secrets you should know about the teacher or the community.

3) How Do You Feel: Do you feel an affinity for the teacher? (Or a similar question if you prefer: Do you feel a connection to the teacher?)

4) Try It On: Make a provisional commitment to the teacher and group, but don't sign on the dotted line.

5) Commit: If, after you've followed the previous suggestions, the situation feels right, then commit to it—knowing there are no guarantees.

Drawing from forty years' experience, I have several suggestions to add to these guidelines. First, do not believe that robes and titles ensure that mentors are enlightened, or even ethical. Second, always look carefully whether the teacher is there for you, or vice versa. Be careful of being used. Third, trust your own gut and intelligence, and don't hesitate to walk away—no matter the circumstances—if the situation doesn't feel right. All these suggestions are helpful, but I'd like to especially reinforce Richard Lewis's "no guarantees" clause. It is not unusual to like a teacher at first, and later find him or her wanting.

All these guidelines don't cover the obverse situation, however, where the teacher seems unfit for the job, but is in fact eminently qualified.

Of my many Dharma teachers, the greatest was Chögyam Trungpa Rinpoche. Rinpoche was a drunkard (he eventually died of alcoholism), smoked, took drugs, and slept with hundreds of women while being married. He was also enlightened, as I found when he transmitted an experience of enlightened mind to me on our first meeting. I quickly felt an affinity for him; receiving enlightenment does that. No teacher in the many years since his death has come close to revealing the Dharma to me as he did. One never knows about teachers, and we must not be quick to reject them without spending time in their company. Certainly, on first look, I would have found that Chögyam Trungpa Rinpoche failed any list of desired qualities in a teacher—and thereby excluded myself from any chance of attaining enlightenment in this lifetime.

Many other great spiritual masters have been seemingly unfit for their role. As mentioned previously, in India, between about 750 CE and 1150 CE, there lived a group of people known as *mahasiddhas* ("great spiritually powerful ones"), who were enlightened and who manifested their attainment in powerful ways. To a casual observer, they would have seemed poor choices for a dharma teacher. Acinta spent his time obsessed with attaining wealth, until he met his guru. Tantepa was a gambler, and attained enlightenment after a particularly nasty loss. Shavaripa made his living as a hunter before seeing the light and attaining advanced Buddhist insight. The point is that it's best to keep an open mind when searching for a teacher.

To begin your search, you can simply Google "renowned dharma teachers," and start reading: about the teachers themselves, and how others feel about them. If people mention that their minds changed in a teacher's presence, pay particular attention.

An authentic teacher can affect our minds in various ways. My wife remembers suddenly feeling more confident in the presence of a teacher. A friend noticed that the water she was drinking had become more delicious, and turned around to see Chögyam Trungpa Rinpoche for the first time.

These kinds of experiences point to a spiritual guide worth considering.

Once we're interested in a mentor, modern transportation makes it simple to arrange a visit. We should realize that, without exaggeration, meeting our teacher can be the most important act of our lives, and other lives to come. In the 11th century CE, Marpa the Translator traveled from Tibet across the Himalayas to India and back three times to be with his guru Naropa. Before his third trip, his wife and students begged him not to go because of his age and the dangers of such an arduous journey. He replied: "No matter what you say, I vowed to meet glorious Naropa once again. Naropa himself advised me to come. Therefore, whatever the consequences may be, I am going to India." (*The Life of Marpa the Translator*, 74.)

Marpa's guru was so important to him that nothing could keep him from seeing Naropa again. Thinking of Marpa, what could possibly prevent us, with access to modern transportation, from meeting a great teacher? Authentic masters have the power to introduce us to the experience of enlightenment, to show us that it is real—not a myth—and that we ourselves can attain it.

In my opinion, the teacher is the single most important aid on the path to enlightenment. He or she, if authentic, will provide everything we need on the journey. For this reason, all serious Buddhist practitioners must do everything in their power to find a living, personal guide who is right for them. Real practitioners are betting their lives on the benefits of the Dharma. They cannot afford the handicap of an absent, unethical, or incompetent teacher.

It is tragic and true that most people who enter the Dharma will never witness enlightenment, much less experience it. For practitioners who sit observing mind year after year, there is nothing that encourages or assists them more than meeting an enlightened teacher.

13

THE TEACHINGS

Some 2,500 hundred years ago, after many trials and errors, Gautama Buddha awakened to the understanding of the true nature of himself and the world. His awakening is the basis of the teachings in what later became known as Buddhism. These teachings are the second indispensable aid on the path, and they act as signposts to help students appreciate where they are on it, and where they have yet to go.

What are the properties of the teachings? First, they are true. They are often referred to as the *Dharma*, a Sanskrit word meaning "truth" or "norm." Dharma may also, depending on context, refer to the Buddha's actual experience, or to all worldly phenomena. In this case, it refers to the teachings on truth; not simply a Buddhist account of truth, but *the* complete and accurate truth about the nature of mind and reality.

Second, the teachings exist for us to experience directly. Buddhism is not a belief system, but a path of direct experience. We begin by believing the teachings, but if we approach the path correctly, over time we begin to actually incorporate their message into our being. As we do so, we make an important discovery: everything we have learned is, to some extent, misleading. We've been hearing all about the taste of water, but when we actually drink water it tastes quite unlike what we expected. Words can never truly impart experience, a truth emphasized by several pithy sayings within the teachings themselves. One is the admonishment "don't eat the menu for the meal," meaning not to confuse simply knowing the teachings with experiencing them. Buddha was also quoted as saying, "I must state clearly that my teaching is a method to experience reality and not reality itself, just as a finger pointing at the moon is not the moon itself" (*Old Path White Clouds*, 211). This is the source of the oft-heard quip, "Don't mistake the finger for the moon."

Even though the teachings are not the experiences themselves, we should not edit or twist them in any way. One pitfall to be avoided is the tendency to reinterpret the teachings to fit our current understanding. The reality is that for most of us, many of the teachings will be incomprehensible for a long time. (The Dharma shares that property with many disciplines, from math to medicine.) However, time and personal experience will eventually show us that the teachings are accurate—we simply have not yet advanced far enough to understand them. In the meantime, we should not become skeptics, or align the teachings to fit our own experientially uninformed concepts. An authentic teacher can be very helpful in this regard.

Speaking of teachers, the Dharma has many forms of transmission beyond written and spoken teachings. I received some of my most helpful instruction in the Dharma simply by watching my teacher, Chögyam Trungpa Rinpoche. For example, I once received an unforgettable teaching on compassion when my teacher, who had a neurological problem, stopped on his way to the bathroom to administer to a woman who stood before him crying. In the process of tending to her, he wet his pants. His commitment to her welfare taught me volumes about compassion. If you have the good fortune to encounter an enlightened being, you will find that his or her every action is instructive—and that some of those instructions will only become apparent years after the fact.

Lastly, the teachings share an overriding theme: they all point to the truth of egolessness. There is a saying in Tibetan Buddhism, "All Dharma agrees at one point." The point on which all Dharma agrees is egolessness: the truth that we, and all objects in the world, have no inherent existence. Self, ego, and "me" are mistakes made by mind, as is the belief that objects in the world are real or have an inherent self-nature. We can think of the teachings as ego poison, which we ingest to prevent ego from destroying our lives. Serious illnesses require serious remedies.

The teachings are indispensable on the path. Without encountering the Dharma, we would never know the possibilities of our human existence. We would never enjoy the beauty of the truth, as clearly and poetically espoused by great teachers. And we would never realize that what we are learning is our own nature.

14

SPIRITUAL PRACTICES

Another support on the path to enlightenment is spiritual practice. Of the many practices in Buddhism, one common to most traditions is mindfulness-awareness meditation.

As the name suggests, this practice has both a mindfulness and an awareness component. The mindfulness aspect involves paying attention, like "minding" a child. In mindfulness meditation, we mind mind. When we do this, body also becomes involved, and it fills with mind. Body becoming "mind full" is another way of thinking about mindfulness. When we're caught up in thoughts and emotions, we leave our bodies, and only through mindfulness does body fill again with mind.

Awareness is the expansion of attention from the object of mindfulness to everything around it: the world of the senses, as well as thoughts and emotions. Awareness allows practitioners to contact the greater world. It also represents the beginning of *prajña*, superior insight, which will later reveal the true nature of mind and reality.

Buddhism has many types of spiritual practices beyond mindfulness-awareness meditation. Some practices in the Vajrayana tradition involve visualizing a deity that represents the enlightened nature of mind, Pure Land Buddhism's main practice is a recitation to the celestial Buddha Amitabha, and so on. Whatever practices we employ, they must all fulfill one criterion: they should not encourage a gaining attitude. Practices designed to help us experience higher planes of consciousness, faster "vibrations," various sounds or lights, or any other goals, blind mind with those goals and prevent it from seeing its true nature.

This applies as well to times when we feel the practice is not working, or that we're not getting anywhere. As the Zen master Shunryu Suzuki Roshi said:

———————

When you are tired of sitting, or when you are disgusted with your practice, you should recognize this as a warning signal. You become discouraged with your practice when your practice has been idealistic. You have some gaining idea in your practice and it is not pure enough. It is when your practice is rather greedy that you become discouraged with it. So you should be grateful that you have a sign or warning signal to show you the weak point in your practice.

Zen Mind, Beginner's Mind, 72.

———————

A gaining attitude isn't our only problem in meditation, especially at first. Most spiritual disciplines are not easy, but mindfulness-awareness practice is particularly difficult for beginners. While visualization practices provide some interest, as does chanting, simply looking at mind itself for long periods is a major test for untrained minds, which continually entertain thoughts and emotions that distract the meditator from the present. Mind shrieks in frustration and groans with boredom, and body tires.

I am reminded of a month-long meditation retreat in which I sat behind a beautiful woman I knew. Over and over, day after day, my mind was stolen from the present by the passion I felt for her. I literally ached each night from the physical strain of my attention going to her throughout the ten-hour days of meditation. It was a long month.

Despite these and other rigors, meditation is a powerful asset to students of Buddhism. One of its gifts is to keep us in the present, rather than occupied by remembrances of the past or hopes and fears of the future. On a prosaic level, being in the moment also helps us avoid unwanted accidents, like stepping in front of a car or missing the next step on the stairs. Being in the present is also mandatory on the path to enlightenment, because only in the present can the true nature of mind be observed. In other words, people consumed by thoughts and emotions about the past or future are missing the mind that is enlightenment.

Meditation also familiarizes us with the workings of mind, and helps us make a relationship with mind itself. As we observe it over time, we notice that thoughts are *just* thoughts: simple occurrences of mind, not activities that can injure us or carry us to unwanted places. Meditation also helps us assume a balanced approach toward mental events, by allowing them to come and go naturally without rejecting or grasping onto them. As a result, meditation practitioners spend less time ruminating, and more time aware of themselves and others.

The more we practice, the more we see. Enlightenment results when the awareness we apply in spiritual practices sees itself. At that point, we realize that meditation is what we are, have always been, and will always be. It's well worth the effort to eventually see what the practices have been showing us all along.

15

SANGHA

*S*angha, a Sanskrit word meaning "community," has several meanings in Buddhism. The monks and nuns in a monastic setting may be called "the sangha," and "the Noble Sangha" is a term used for enlightened beings. However, sangha as I'll use it here, and as most Western practitioners will experience it, is simply the community of students within a Buddhist tradition: a group of mostly lay practitioners, living in the workaday world, who follow a particular teacher and body of teachings.

Sanghas vary in accord with the type of Buddhism they practice. Members of Zen sanghas tend to follow the Japanese mannerisms of the teachers who brought Zen to Western shores: they are generally quite disciplined, taciturn, and prone to end Dharma discussions of any length with a stifling Zen saying or the admonition to "just sit." In Vajrayana Buddhism, the community tends to be more talkative and convivial. Advanced Vajrayana practitioners engage in ceremonial feasts where alcohol is served, where they converse at length and read spiritual poems and pithy instructions from renowned teachers.

Although sanghas have different styles, each sangha seems to find a balance if its members practice, read the teachings, and respect the teacher. Chögyam Trungpa Rinpoche discusses this balance as follows:

———

The concept of sangha, for instance, means a group of people working together as brothers and sisters, working together as spiritual friends to one another. That is an important point. In order to be brothers and sisters, you have to be open to each other as well. Being open is not being dependent on others, which blocks their openness. In other words, the sangha does not create a situation of claustrophobia for each person in it. If somebody falls, you will stand independently; because you are not leaning on the other person, you don't fall. When one person falls it doesn't create a chain reaction of other people falling as well. So independence is equally important as being together, acting as an inspiration to one another.

The Collected Works of Chögyam Trungpa 6, 151.

———

A healthy sangha brings many practical benefits. Sangha members can pool funds to lease or buy spaces for group practice—or, in smaller sanghas, take turns practicing in one another's homes. A sangha can gather the resources, logistics, and enough people to invite spiritually advanced teachers, and enjoy the benefit of their presence and teachings. Sangha members also naturally form strong social connections with one another.

These practical benefits can be life-changing. The greatest single gift any sangha has provided me was Karmê Chöling, a Buddhist meditation center where I lived for two years. My teacher's sangha bought it for him, and I had the good fortune to live there at a very trying time in my life. It gave me an easy job, the freedom to practice hours of meditation, and a community of practitioners who were all crazy in their own way—like me. There I met and received teachings from my teacher, and from some of the greatest Tibetan Buddhist and Zen teachers of the time. The period I spent there set me firmly on the path that I have continued to the present day.

In addition to these practical benefits, a healthy sangha can directly confer numerous spiritual benefits, some straightforward and some more esoteric. At the commonsense level, many people find meditating in a group much less wearing, and much easier to commit to, than sitting alone every day. The sangha also provides a mirror that reveals our problems. If we consistently encounter animosity, we are probably generating it. If we find ourselves being repeatedly overlooked for positions within the sangha, it may be because we are looking only to our own interests. It's not always easy to peer into the sangha's mirror, but if we are open enough, we can learn a lot about where we're stuck.

Also—and this must be experienced rather than read—the true nature of mind becomes more prominent and accessible when people sit together. How this happens I have no idea, being a telepathy skeptic, but unquestionably a mental aura of some type arises.

Lastly, the sangha acts as a conduit for the blessings of an ancient lineage of enlightened beings. Practitioners benefit not only from the living but also from the dead. Like one candle lighting another through the ages, lineage transmits the light of realization down to the living sangha. To students who are open to the lineage's power, the great ones of the past can provide much-needed assistance on the path.

Having listed all these benefits, we must also remember that lay sanghas are composed of people with egos.

Of all the manifestations of ego I experienced in sanghas, the most glaring were ethical transgressions. In the Buddhist groups I've been a part of, the teachers, teachings, and practices were generally good, but a recurring theme was nonadherence to basic Buddhist ethics, such as: refraining from taking what is not given, sexual misconduct, lying, misusing drugs or alcohol, and killing. With regard to killing, I know of two occasions in my sangha where knives were drawn. As for the other precepts, they were continually and casually disregarded.

I myself was, among other things, robbed (both personally and as a group member), painfully manipulated, lied to, embarrassed, and excluded from group positions for political reasons. Other students committed these transgressions in the course of vying for proximity to the teacher, jockeying for promotion, seeking money, and pursuing various kinds of sexual fulfillment. My own stupidity also contributed, by making me an easy target for others' schemes.

Do not assume anything about a sangha's students, and especially about students in positions of authority. Sanghas contain some wonderful people, and some less than wonderful people. I entered my teacher's sangha quite naïvely, and for a time I believed that his students shared his magic, especially the senior ones.

I suffered some shocking discoveries in the process of being disabused of that idea.

As I review my life in the Dharma, I feel that the sangha has been a real trial, and also a blessing—and that, all in all, the blessings have been greater. In fact, blessings often arose from the trials.

16

LIFE

In addition to the teacher, teachings, practices, and sangha, we now turn to a major and seldom-mentioned aid on the Buddhist path: life itself.

Buddha's First Noble Truth states that life is pervaded with suffering. Life also contains pleasure, but even that pleasure carries the seed of suffering: *How can I get more of this?*, *What if this stops?*, and so on. And so life, as we conventionally experience it, is tedious.

Confronted with the pain of life, and with its brevity, humans have devised numerous conceptual schemes to ease our minds. Religions speak of heaven, being with God for eternity. (Even Buddhism has sects that continually repeat a mantra to take them to the "Pure Land" when they die.) As for nonbelievers, they assume their own attitudes to give context to their existence: "Life is what you make it," "You'll never get out of life alive," "Eat, drink and be merry," and the great pitcher Satchel Paige's admonition: "Don't look back; something might be gaining on you."

These efforts notwithstanding, the truth is that pain is not something to fantasize or explain away. My experience, shared with practitioners through the ages, is that painful life circumstances can bring spiritual insight more readily than years of meditative practices. Life's ups and downs played a key role in my spiritual progress through the years. On one occasion, after many years of severe job-induced stress, I sat on a bed, relaxed for a moment, and realized that I had no self. Some years later, following a heartbreaking personal disappointment, I suddenly intuited emptiness.

Similarly, many past masters came to key insights as a result of life's tests. The Tibetan saint Milarepa went out to collect firewood while on solitary retreat. A sudden storm arose with a great wind that blew away the wood he had accumulated, and tore his threadbare clothing off before he passed out.

––––––––––

When he came to, the storm was over. High up on the branch of a tree he saw a shred of his clothing swaying in the gentle breeze. The utter futility of this world and all its affairs struck Milarepa, and a strong feeling of renunciation

116

overwhelmed him. Sitting down upon a rock, he meditated once more.

The Hundred Thousand Songs of Milarepa, 1.

Another example is the 17th-century Zen master Bankei, who, in his own words, describes attaining enlightenment while deathly ill with tuberculosis:

I felt a strange sensation in my throat. I spat against a wall. A mass of black phlegm, large as a soapberry, rolled down the side... Suddenly just at that instant... I realized what it was that had escaped me until now: All things are perfectly resolved in the Unborn.

Unborn, 10.

Milarepa's Dharma heir, Gampopa, decided to become a Buddhist monk after losing his wife and child to a plague. The list goes on.

The pain we feel in life is unsurpassed in its ability to get our attention, or to force us to give up and drop into unexpected realities. Relinquishing a long period of psychological torment can leave mind bare just long enough to see its emptiness. So can impending death, such as Bankei faced. Of course, no sane person likes to suffer, but it is simply the case that worldly suffering often leads to insight. People at the end of their rope are the most likely to let go, and fall into the true nature of things.

Although pain is a fact of life, Buddhism considers life itself to be an important, rare, and valuable gift. In fact, Buddhists often speak of a "precious human birth" as one of the greatest gifts possible. Only within this human life can we experience the true nature of mind and reality, and help others do the same. Buddhists also believe in reincarnation, and that to be born a human is extremely rare. Buddha mentions an ox yoke floating in the ocean, and states that it's more likely that a blind turtle who surfaces once every hundred years would stick its head through the yoke, than that we would have attained a human birth in this lifetime.

Understanding the rarity and importance of human existence causes us to view life differently. Human life is short, and we have a monumental task before us. We need to attain enlightenment in this lifetime, or there are no guarantees where we will end up in the next. Also, only as an enlightened human can we best help others, in this existence and thereafter. If we take the Buddhist teachings seriously, life's brevity will not merely frighten or depress us, but spur us along the path to enlightenment.

Lastly, if we do attain enlightenment in this lifetime, life takes on a completely different aspect. We now experience that life and death don't exist, obviating concerns about rebirth. Mind—what we truly are, or aren't—is seen to be immortal, as well as always now, and vested with loving-kindness and compassion. Even though, as the "nows" pile up, the body steadily deteriorates and its impending death becomes ever more apparent, the mind that inhabits it is not fazed. This description is not Buddhist dogma, but how an enlightened mind feels.

Very few of us view life as a rare and precious opportunity to transcend our ideas about enlightenment, and to become enlightenment itself. Fewer still bet their lives on accomplishing that. These few, although their time is short and the task most difficult, are not disheartened. They have learned that they are going to suffer, and that no concept of a savior can help them, so they might as well face life and use its pain to their advantage. Whether they find enlightenment or not, in the end they respect themselves for having approached life bravely and correctly.

EVERYDAY CONSIDERATIONS ON THE PATH

17

SANITY

Sanity may seem an odd subject to mention on the path to enlightenment. On the other hand, greater sanity exists than is generally known in the West. In fact, enlightenment is the attainment of the greatest sanity, because it transcends beliefs about self and the world that have caused humanity ceaseless and inestimable suffering through the ages.

I feel especially qualified to write about sanity as a part of the Buddhist path. My credentials include having been unsane in the conventional Western sense due to a serious mood disorder; sane in this same sense thanks to medication; a recipient of the transcendental sanity of Buddhism, known as realization; and, lastly, a witness to insane sanity, or *crazy wisdom* (Tibetan, *yeshe cholwa*), in the person of my guru. In this chapter, I'll outline my journey through these stages of sanity.

In the West, a loose definition of a sane person is someone who thinks and behaves in a rational manner. Of course, everyone has glitches, but well-defined criteria exist for what we consider sane. One of the best ways to understand these criteria is to learn what sanity is not, and the West has done just that, most notably in the core psychology reference manual the *Diagnostic and Statistical Manual of Mental Disorders* (DSM).

I have the dubious distinction of fulfilling the criteria for one of the DSM's maladies, listed under the mood disorders as major depression. Since my early thirties (I'm now 77) it has shadowed me, and it has come close to killing me on a number of occasions. I find the nature of major depression best defined by William Styron, an excellent writer and fellow sufferer:

The pain of depression is quite unimaginable to those who have not suffered it, and it kills in many instances because its anguish can no longer be borne. The prevention of many suicides will continue to be hindered until there is a general awareness of the nature of this pain.

Darkness Visible: A Memoir of Madness, 33.

When my struggle with major depression began, it slowly crept over me, covering the natural space and awareness of my mind. I turn to William Styron again to describe the experience:

The madness of depression is, generally speaking, the antithesis of violence. It is a storm indeed, but a storm of murk. Soon evident are sloweddown responses, near paralysis, psychic energy throttled back close to zero. Ultimately the body is affected and feels sapped, drained.

Darkness Visible: A Memoir of Madness, 25.

In my case, I turned to Buddhism to help me with the "murk" of depression. It helped, but it also proved dangerous, as I flirted with suicide by depending solely on it as therapy. More specifically, my practice helped me with my illness as long as I could do enough meditation—which was five hours a day at a live-in meditation center. When I returned to everyday life, however, my depression worsened due to stress and decreased meditation time, and I wandered toward the cliff's edge. Relief came only when I finally made my own diagnosis, and began antidepressant therapy which saved my life. Most people with my problem can't or won't do five hours of meditation each day, so they require more than Buddhism to help them.

In fact, with some mental illnesses, meditation is more of a hindrance than a help. One example comes from my time living at a Buddhist meditation center in Vermont called Karmê Chöling. As a newcomer, I lived in the men's dorm, as did the visiting meditators, so I observed many of them as they came through the programs. On one occasion, I noticed that a visitor was acting strangely after several days of meditation, and I informed one of the directors of the center, who listened to my account with minimal interest. Early one morning several days later, I awoke to find that the dorm was very cold; it was winter, and a door to the outside was open. It dawned on me that the person I had been concerned about had exited the dorm only in bed clothes into several feet of Vermont snow and zero-degree temperatures. I ascended to the well-appointed room of the director and told him what had happened, and a successful search was initiated. Some forty years later, it is now recognized that prolonged meditation worsens certain types of mental disorders.

When I began taking depression medication, I came to understand how sick I had really been, and how risky it had been for me to depend only on Buddhism for relief. Medication also provided an added effect as it dispelled my depression and brought me to the level of Western sanity. I had the good fortune to notice that many of the Buddhist teachings I had learned were manifesting themselves as I improved. One of the most noticeable effects was an increase in mental space. Until then, it had seemed like I lived in a tent, but with treatment, the flap suddenly opened and I could see the world. The medication was helping me progress along the Dharmic path. Of course, I still had an ego and all the rest, but I saw enough from being properly medicated to know that the Buddhist path was true—and doable.

The major lesson I learned from my long experience with mental illness, though, was that we must attain conventional sanity before attempting the greater sanity of Buddhism. Based on my own life experience, I now advocate that all debilitating mental disorders be referred to Western-based professionals before the sufferers turn to spirituality as therapy.

Once Western sanity was established, I then turned to the greater sanity of Buddhist insight. Although reading this may provoke resentment, the truth is that all human beings who lack Buddhist insight suffer from a serious and multifaceted mental disorder. To believe in a self and bow to its demands is the most prevalent and debilitating mental affliction known. Self engenders constant psychological pain through wanting, rejecting, and ignoring what it feels to be separate from itself. Our certainty that the world is real is another painful delusion, because this heavy realness oppresses us. Only through Buddhist insight may we dispel these mental disorders, and find the true sanity of an undivided, limitless world that is calm, peaceful, restful, loving, and effortlessly aware.

An advanced stage of Buddhism's transcendental sanity is the experience known as vajra being. When practitioners experience emptiness, they have the requisite insight to enter the Vajrayana, or *Vajra* (Sanskrit, "Indestructible") *Yana* (Sanskrit, "Vehicle"), and vajra being is one of the fruitions of that yana. Chögyam Trungpa describes vajra being as follows:

It brings an experience of complete indestructibility that is unchallengeable, immovable and completely solid. The experience of indestructibility can only occur when we realize that nonexistence is possible.

The Pocket Chögyam Trungpa, 60.

With vajra being, we enter a new stage of sanity, and discover a mind that is not influenced by stresses of any type. Vajra mind is the ultimate mental power, immune to any energies that may disturb its tranquility. Personal power in much of society implies wealth or an elevated position: being intelligent or charismatic, having physical strength, or having further qualities that allow us to influence others. These attributes are only simulacra of power. Real power arises from understanding what we and the world really are, which is nothing.

Nothing—or, more precisely, emptiness—is the greatest power that humans can possess. Even intellectually, we can understand that no force affects nothing, and the same is true with the experience of the emptiness of mind. From the experience of emptiness, vajra being develops with time and practice. We know we are beginning to experience it when previously strong energies are defanged by mind. We already are the emptiness and awareness of mind, but now energies such as fear, anger, or wanting emerge from that mind and quickly and effortlessly merge back into it. What is left is the feeling of the unruffled vastness of realized mind, naturally prepared for whatever comes next.

In my experience, vajra being does not erect an indestructible wall around me that nothing can penetrate, but is an empty vastness where occurrences of mind naturally dissipate. When I began feeling vajra being, I noticed its effect especially in my everyday life—which is generally a good indicator of our progress on the path. In particular, I became more generous and patient. I wasn't as rushed, because I felt more capable of handling misfortune, knowing that events would not stick and continue cycling in vajra being the way they did in confused mind. Since I no longer felt that I had to jump on events immediately to control them, I began allowing them to mature, often with surprisingly good results.

Feeling indestructible made me much less needy as well. I didn't have to clutch on to what I had; I was now vajra being no matter what happened, and I could afford to share my possessions with others. The loveliest part of vajra being I found was that, along with its unceasing power, it was so secure and rich that its sole motivation was to help others. This great power, by its nature, did not suppress others but nourished them.

To me, the experience was a really big leap, and one I feel very fortunate to have realized. However, vajra being is not a one-shot affair; it unfolds continually as we become more confident in dealing with greater energies. Meditation is particularly important in this respect, because it supplies a controlled environment in which we can watch energies dispel in mind, preparing us for the buffeting the world is certain to provide.

One would think that my journey to sanity was complete after realizing Buddhist insight—and it would have been, except for my meeting Chögyam Trungpa Rinpoche, a Vajrayana guru in the crazy wisdom tradition. For various reasons, one being that I loved him, I saw early on that he not only radiated enlightenment, but he also manifested crazy wisdom. This is a yet higher level of Buddhist sanity, attained by only a few of the most advanced Vajrayana teachers. (In Tibet, as it happens, my teacher's lineage was specifically renowned for crazy wisdom.)

Crazy wisdom is better defined as "wisdom crazy," since it is a level of sanity so advanced that those without it see it as crazy. Chögyam Trungpa himself is the perfect person to describe it:

———————

Crazy wisdom is absolute perceptiveness, with fearlessness and bluntness. Fundamentally it is being wise but not holding to particular doctrines or disciplines or formats. There aren't any books to follow. Rather there is endless spontaneity taking place. There is room for being blunt, room for being open. That openness is created by the environment itself. In fact, at the level of crazy wisdom, all activity is created by the environment. The crazy wisdom person is just an activator, just one of the conditions that have evolved in the environment.

The Collected Works of Chögyam Trungpa, vol. 4, 131-132.

One time during my stay at Karmê Chöling, Rinpoche visited. While giving an evening talk, he began choking. Being a physician, I came to his aid. It was there that I first saw crazy wisdom in action, as his dying—and he *was* dying, for a short spell—ended up creating a special Dharmic atmosphere. A sense of awake immediately arose in his students, and fear for his life generated devotion in them, both necessary ingredients for their progress on the path. For my part, the crisis allowed me to be physically close to him, and to feel the preciousness he emanated. *Rinpoche* means "precious one" in Tibetan, and to my surprise I discovered that one could actually feel his preciousness when near him. Additionally, my total commitment to saving him connected my heart to his, and that connection has been of daily importance to me in the years that followed.

Another example of my teacher's crazy wisdom is a particularly well-known story in his sangha that I did not witness. Its background was that Rinpoche visited an area to teach, and along the way he decided with his entourage to have a drink in a rather seedy bar. He had recently acquired a water gun, and he began squirting the waitress with it, who eventually stopped being amused and complained. On departing, he hit a pool player's cue on purpose as the player took a shot. In short, he was not ingratiating himself with a rough-looking crowd. A member of Rinpoche's party recounts what followed as they left the bar:

Out in the parking lot, after we had all gotten into the car with the windows open on a warm summer's night, a man approached from out of the gloom with a rifle in his hand that he trained on Rinpoche, who was sitting in the front passenger's seat. I was sitting directly behind him, looking up the barrel of a gun and I clearly heard the man say, "I'm going to fucking blow your head off, you fucking chink bastard."

Silence. Mind stops. Wide awake. Nobody moves, A drawn-out pause.

Rinpoche replies, "Go ahead, shoot."

I'm thinking that this may be my last moment on earth. Then Rinpoche draws his own weapon and commences to shoot the would-be shooter with squirts from his water pistol while repeating,

"Go ahead, shoot," and "Are you chicken?"

The rifle man seems stunned, is speechless, immobile, a looming vivid menace, but without any substance or action.

After a time our driver decides that it's okay to put the car in gear and we slowly exit the parking lot, returning up the hill to the retreat center, now all dark, shuttered and silent, late on this peaceful summer's night.

David Wilde, The Chronicles of Chögyam Trungpa Rinpoche

What is one to make of this account? To me, the encounter has all the ingredients of crazy wisdom. The first is fearlessness, in this case to an incomprehensible degree, which is one reason why there are so few crazy wisdom people. Chögyam Trungpa Rinpoche was, from everything I saw and heard, completely fearless. Bluntness was also on display with his taunting to shoot. And, of course, the whole affair was not orchestrated but spontaneous, with Rinpoche simply acting as an element the environment created. One of the eerie things about crazy wisdom is how one sees that it is not planned, but simply happens—yet one is never certain if that is really the case.

Another clear crazy wisdom element in this story is the responses others had to the episode. Traditionally, three occasions are especially opportune for experiencing enlightened mind: at death, during orgasm, and while an accident is unfolding. The people in the car with Rinpoche were experiencing the third, as the narrator makes clear with the words "silence," "mind stops," and "wide awake." These are aspects of enlightened mind, and whether they recognized it as such—and whether it continued—is not recorded. Nevertheless, that was the wisdom created during the terrifying craziness.

And lastly, what happened to the gunman? Having seen this happen to both myself and others on a number of occasions, my sense is that he suddenly encountered the nature of Rinpoche's mind, and as a result became "speechless," "immobile," without "action," and, most interestingly, without "substance." Of all the words the narrator could use, why did he choose "substance," when "without substance" is precisely how emptiness makes objects appear? Was he experiencing emptiness while staring at the gunman, and was the gunman transfixed by Rinpoche's enlightened mind? Was the whole crazy encounter actually an enlightenment party for all concerned? As always, there aren't any definite answers with crazy wisdom.

So, these are the levels of sanity I have seen. I have experienced Western unsanity and sanity; Buddhism's greater sanity; and, finally, crazy sanity. One result is that I have developed a rather inclusive sense of what is sane, and I am not so quick to decide who is and isn't *compos mentis*. I am reminded of an anecdote about Chögyam Trungpa Rinpoche and Dilgo Khyentse Rinpoche, both beings at the highest levels of Buddhist attainment. They once had a discussion about their level of realization, and they came to an agreement. They decided that they were "equally crazy."

18

INTELLECT

Having discussed sanity, we now turn to another aspect of mind, intellect, as part of the path to enlightenment. The relationship between sanity and intellect brings a story to mind. A man was driving a truck past a mental institution one day, when the truck's top became stuck on the entrance to an underpass. Getting out of the truck to look at the problem, the man noticed a mental patient standing behind the institution's fence observing him. The driver could not figure out how to free the truck. Eventually, the mental patient said, "Why don't you let air out of the tires?" The driver, astounded at the patient's solution, asked him, "What are you doing in there?" The patient replied, "I'm crazy, not stupid."

Enlightenment requires intellect. To progress in the Dharma, students must learn, and contemplate what they have learned. Since reasoning through and understanding the teachings comes more easily to intellectually gifted people than to others, those people often teach the Dharma, introducing others to it and explaining its logics. Intelligent people exert considerable influence over beginners—and over more advanced students, as well—so their expertise is very important to the sangha.

In my experience, intellects also have a natural attraction to the teachings. I have found that people who master rigorous intellectual disciplines easily are attracted to disciplines they find challenging. They regard what they don't understand as a problem to be solved—and the Dharma certainly fills that role.

Also, the Dharma is attractive to intelligent people because of its emphasis on direct experience rather than on unsupported beliefs, an emphasis they also find appealing in math and science. Buddha was a brilliant man who used mind to study mind. He sat in meditation and examined mind for years before he discovered its true nature. Like a scientist, he did not rely on the beliefs of others or on received wisdom, but on his own research. Buddhism remains to this day fundamentally experiential and not belief-based, and this emphasis attracts intelligent people.

While intellect has its place in the Dharma, there are areas it cannot enter. The benefits of ratiocination can never establish Dharma's actual feeling—in fact, they can inhibit it. In a somewhat ironic twist, Lodro

Thaye, a legendary 19th-century Tibetan intellect, makes this point:

Since in the view of mahamudra [enlightenment]

Analysis does not apply,

Cast mind-made knowledge far away.

The Rain of Wisdom, 90.

This is easier said than done. It is much easier to learn the Dharma than to be it, and as a result students who intellectually know the Dharma are much more prevalent than practitioners who experience it.

An intelligent person can assimilate the important Dharmic teachings rather quickly, be noticed for his or her intelligence, and join the legion of Dharma teachers who are learned but not realized. Since almost no one experiences Buddhism directly, intellectuals are in little danger of being exposed, so their positions are secure. To acquire insight in the Dharma, on the other hand, takes unshakeable determination and effort, usually over many years. Moreover, practitioners seeking insight run the added risk of having it elude them throughout their lifetime—unlike intelligent people, who are more or less born that way.

This is not a recent problem. More than a millennium ago, Milarepa, an enlightened being, caused such distress among the Buddhist logicians of his time with his actual experience of the Dharma that one of them poisoned him to death.

The intelligent dominate much of the Dharma, but the insightful are its heart's blood, because only they know what the words really mean. All the concepts promulgated in Dharmic groups around the world are based on actual experience, and they only come to life with that experience. For example, it is lovely to explain to a rapt group that we are the world and it is us—but not if we personally have no clue what that statement means. To actually see in each moment that we really are the chair, door, or tree we observe is a form of understanding that far exceeds any concepts we may have about it. Similarly, to effortlessly see that the table we are typing on, although solid and hard, is also form inseparable from emptiness far exceeds any hint one gets from reading or hearing about form and emptiness.

Intellect has its place, but it can never take us into the world of enlightened experience. In fact, the very act of filling our mind with ideas about what is real greatly inhibits us from experiencing it. The more we conceptualize about the Dharma, the further we drift from it. Reality is mind, and mind cannot be seen when cluttered with concepts about itself.

The first time I picked up a book by Chögyam Trungpa Rinpoche, I couldn't understand what he was saying; it was "all Tibetan to me." The same was true of the writings of other recognized Buddhist teachers. Fortunately for me, instead of discarding Buddhism as nonsense, I became curious about *why* I couldn't understand it. I then took a step back, looked at my dilemma critically, and made several determinations.

First, I was not too dumb to understand Buddhism. Although I knew that parts of advanced math and physics were permanently beyond me, I had enough experience mastering other disciplines, especially medicine, to know my capabilities. I also would not believe that all those people who experienced enlightenment for thousands of years were making it up or insane—and I sensed, correctly, that what they had discovered was the pinnacle of human existence. Moreover, not long after beginning in the Dharma, I came to the conclusion that there was no way to figure it out logically. After all, how can one understand concepts like "form is emptiness," "there is no self," and "the world is really unreal"? There had to be another way, and there was: one had to become it.

After arriving at that conclusion, I devoted myself to the intuitive approach, sitting long hours in meditation, and spending as much time as I could in the presence of my teacher. I had resolved that learning the teachings was not enough for me. I had to experience them.

Intellect is helpful on the path to enlightenment. It makes us aware of the topic of enlightenment, and it helps us understand the steps involved in attaining it. Books, lectures, and other pursuits continue our interest in Buddhism. Intellect is also the perfect complement to actual experience as we progress in the Dharma. We can hear about reality, contemplate what we've heard, and then confirm through direct experience that what we learned was accurate. However, we must always be sure not to depend on knowledge to the exclusion of experience.

Of course, the ideal solution is to combine intelligence with insight, and some practitioners have done that to a remarkable degree. Recently I was reading the Dharma when I came upon a quote by the Kagyu Buddhist lineage holder Gampopa: "The ultimate is free of itself." In that instant, I felt the jolt of witnessing great insight meeting great intellect. Gampopa wrote that quote almost a thousand years ago, and it is still as fresh and true as the day he wrote it. We owe a lot to those masters who have reached the pinnacle of insight—and then, from that pinnacle, employed brilliant minds to explain it to us.

19

REST

fter reading about self-existing awareness, vajra being, and crazy wisdom, a simple topic like rest might seem out of place. But the fact is, rest is a constant and important part of the Buddhist path, and it manifests in unexpected and helpful ways. Shang Rinpoche gives us a sense of the importance of rest to meditation:

A relaxed mind is all that is necessary. Perfect meditation will arise in a perfectly relaxed mind. A middling meditation will arise in a semi-relaxed mind. The least kind of meditation will arise in the least relaxed mind.

Mahamudra and Related Instructions, 78.

It's helpful to know, as a start, that effort plays a different role in the world of insight than in the everyday world. In the usual world, effort is how we solve problems; but in the enlightened one, effort *creates* problems, by intruding on the unobstructed nature of enlightened mind.

This statement, counterintuitive as usual, raises the question of how we can live without earning money, buying groceries, caring for loved ones, and everything else that life demands. And that question brings us back to rest itself—because if we really know how to rest mind, we can do all those things and rest at the same time.

So how do we rest? The answer is not a sandy beach and palm trees or billions in the bank, but by divesting ourselves of attachments. We don't have to buy airline tickets or start a hedge fund to rest mind; we can do it in each moment, by sitting in meditation and relaxing our attachments to the thoughts and emotions that disturb us. Then, we can go shopping with a mind that is completely unruffled by parking, checkout lines, and so on. When we learn how to recognize and drop attachments, we can rest under all circumstances.

When we attempt to divorce ourselves from grasping, however, the problem we immediately face is that *trying* to eliminate grasping creates an attachment to eliminating it. This dilemma reminds me of a statement I heard early in the Dharma, and of which I grew tired: "We already are what we seek." I always thought, *What does it matter if we are, if we can't find it?* Nevertheless, as galling as hearing it repeated is, the statement is true. We already are rest, and to find it we simply have to let go of attachments, and not try to push them away.

The best way to do that is—you guessed it— meditation. Using mindfulness-awareness practice, we begin to shift from our preoccupations with thoughts, emotions, and other activities of mind and effortlessly return to the present. Each time we do so, we rest; in fact, we may even feel our body relax as we come back. If we observe closely, we also discover that returning from grasping happens naturally, without any element of effort or trying. We begin to see that both returning to and being in the now are restful, and that wrestling with our attachments is really what stresses us.

In all this, the real villain is our karma. For a very long time, our approach to life has been to try. We continue this pattern in Buddhism, striving to learn and understand new terms, new rituals, and new ways to interact with others and with the teacher. All this takes effort—which we later learn is harmful to our progress. It doesn't seem fair; after all, "we are doing the best we can."

From a Dharmic perspective, however, we are reinforcing our karma, and that is an activity not suited to the Dharma, as Suzuki Roshi makes clear:

If you are trying to attain enlightenment, you are creating and being driven by karma, and you are wasting your time on your black cushion.

Zen Mind, Beginner's Mind, 99.

Because of the power of our karma, at the beginning of our journey on the Buddhist path we exert great effort to learn how to rest. For example, we may wish to see the true nature of mind so that we can find peace, and so we apply ourselves assiduously to meditation, practicing it over and over, year after year. Fortunately, with meditation, we have chosen the best approach to resting. Even though our motivation is flawed, the method we've picked is working unobtrusively to our benefit. Unbeknownst to us, our efforts are setting a trap for ego, the source of our inability to rest.. Ego is trying as hard as it can—employing Dharmic methods designed to remove ego. As it searches for insight, it meditates more, studies the Dharma further, and bonds more closely with the teacher, all activities that lead to its eventual demise and the emergence of restfulness.

Meditation shows us that all our efforts don't work. We continue to return to the places that restrict our freedom, such as overwhelming emotions or selfish endeavors. At some point, practice awakens us enough to realize that trying is ineffectual—or maybe worse than ineffectual, increasing our crankiness, puffing us up with how hard we practice, or making us arrogant about what we've learned. Finally, we see that attaining enlightenment cannot be done, and we give up and just rest in the present. When we relax, and mind is cleared of striving, it begins to see itself more clearly. We start to get somewhere by going nowhere.

At that point, we begin to relinquish our egocentric approach to the Dharma and to relax; and that allows us, at last, to obtain a clearer view of the mind we have been attempting to see. The Dharma has no equal in fooling ego. When it is successful, we discover mind and the restfulness it contains.

In my own life, I spent many years practicing the Dharma so that I could rest my mind from its constant worries. Meditating in this way worked sometimes— and sometimes it caused me to struggle more, as sitting and watching concerns arise again and again intensified them. For a long period, not even meditation guaranteed me restfulness. Desperate for enlightenment to rescue me from my psychological struggles, I endured years of chronic irritation, with ego trying to attain enlightenment and judging its progress. It was a constant, nagging presence that never relented.

All this effort was not wasted, though, because it proved to me that I would never be able to find enlightenment by searching. After twenty years, I finally gave up, and I found what I was seeking—and with it, rest, both in meditation and life.

Up to this point, we have been discussing rest from the unenlightened viewpoint, and have found it difficult to accomplish. With enlightenment, the situation couldn't be more different. Enlightenment is effortless, so rest need not be sought. Self has long since disappeared, along with other, and we have become the world, so we no longer have to deal with the feeling of the world opposing us. We can relax.

We have become a limitless space, without borders to inhibit us or anything outside to influence us. Also, since we are empty, nothing can impact us; and being eternal, we require no maintenance. We don't have to do anything, because we are everything. We no longer try to listen or see, because we *are* listening and seeing themselves, and every other experience that occurs. We are a space that knows and observes;

thoughts and emotions ripple within that space, and then the space returns to itself. We are like a waterfall, which doesn't work at falling but simply does what waterfalls do. Enlightenment is what we truly are and always have been, but didn't realize. As such, we don't have to work at being it, and can simply rest in what we have realized.

Even at this point of advanced insight, we will be surprised to find that we still have not learned to rest completely. Despite being all the qualities of enlightenment just mentioned, we still leave that insight at times—and this causes us to *work* at staying in enlightenment, perhaps by paying more attention to body, the outbreath, or the distance of our gaze. We are still trying to drive the car of enlightenment, even though there is no we and no car.

This car metaphor is not mine, but comes to me from my teacher. At a talk he gave many years ago, I recall raising my hand to ask a question. (I wanted to be a star pupil, so I was asking questions, and of course he effortlessly read what my ego was doing, as only someone without one can.) He smiled, pointed over my head to a woman behind me, and asked her if she ever noticed the road coming to her.

Thirty-five years after my teacher's comment, I was meditating, and suddenly mind quit being "there," and started coming to me. At that point, I knew what my teacher had meant by the road coming to us, and I understood the gift he had offered me years before. With it, I learned complete rest. Through all the insights I have mentioned throughout this book, there had always been the subtle taint of something being *done*. Now, insights were no longer being done; they were doing me.

When we stop driving down the road, and the road starts coming to us, adjustments to the car are no longer required. The road decides where we go, and the road is everything. In other words, all of life is coming to us now, and we don't have to do anything about it—just relax and enjoy the view. We are completely free from all trying, and there is only resting under all circumstances.

Rest is indispensable on both sides of enlightenment. We need rest to reach insight, and rest is a major element of insight itself. We are enlightenment—that is our true nature as a human—and we are meant to find total restfulness in that nature. However, in another bit of Dharmic illogic, we will have to work to relax. Only by working through mind's obstacles will we find the way to complete freedom and restfulness.

20

CONCLUSION

Life is pervaded with suffering, as the Buddha
said 2,500 years ago. In the time since,
enlightenment has proven the only complete
and lasting treatment for that suffering. Only by
realizing the nonexistence of self, the unreality of the
world, and the nonduality of the two—along with the
other insights mentioned in this book—can humans
be relieved of life's stigmata.

With the appearance of global climate change and
the ensuing shrinkage of livable land, resource wars,
unlivable heat, rising sea levels, acidification of
the oceans, drought, starvation, worsening natural
catastrophes, loss of earth's flora and fauna, a
burgeoning of refugees, and previously unheard-of
diseases, suffering is predicted to increase for billions
on the planet in the years to come. The mental
stresses of living will increase as well, along with
alcohol, recreational drugs, and other destructive

means to relieve them. We and our forebears, through ignorance of who we and the world truly are, bear the disgrace for what is happening to the planet, and those who follow will remember us in that way. They will know we have left them the dregs of what was once a beautiful, fruitful planet, which we evolved with and which was suited to us as no other can be. For all the hardship we are leaving them, in recompense, we can at least preserve the authentic path to enlightenment. We have destroyed the perfection of their worldly home, but we can at least save them the perfection of their home in mind.

Although much has been made of other life in the universe, at this point, none has been found. (Perhaps what is out there is too smart to contact us.) The presence of billions of galaxies weighs heavily in favor of other life existing; nevertheless, at this point we remain the only known creatures who experience enlightened mind. Humans may be the only holders of the true nature of reality in the universe. As such, it is incumbent upon us to realize mind, and see that it is perpetuated. If that insight is lost, the universe will have no one to appreciate and understand itself, and with it will be lost the brilliant awareness, beauty, endless freedom, joy, and unconditional love that is it and us.

Essentially, the Dharma has one goal, and that is to benefit others. As I have endeavored to show in this book, enlightenment exists, and we can attain it. We can transmute the pain of existence, and realize the perfection that we are, as related by Nyoshul Khen Rinpoche:

The Mind of the Buddhas

Profound and tranquil, free from complexity,
Uncompounded luminous clarity,
Beyond the mind of conceptual ideas;
This is the depth of the mind of the
Victorious Ones.

In this there is not a thing to be removed,
Nor anything that needs to be added.
It is merely the immaculate
Looking naturally at itself.

The Pocket Tibetan Buddhism Reader, 163.

I would like to thank you for reading this book. It is my fervent wish that you become the qualities it outlines, both for your benefit, and for a world that badly needs your help.

INDEX

WORKS CITED

Chadwick, David. *Crooked Cucumber: The Life and Teaching of Shunryu Suzuki*. Harmony, 2000.

Chang, Garma C.C. *The Hundred Thousand Songs of Milarepa*. Shambhala Publications, 1999.

Lhalungpa, Lobsang, trans. *The Life of Milarepa*. Shambhala Publications, 1985.

Nhat Hanh, Thich. Old Path White Clouds: Walking in the Footsteps of the Buddha. Parallax Press, 1991.

Ray, Reginald. *Indestructible Truth: The Living Spirituality of Tibetan Buddhism*. Shambhala Publications, 2002.

Ray, Reginald. *The Pocket Tibetan Buddhism Reader*. Shambhala Publications, 2004.

Ray, Reginald. *Secrets of the Vajra World: The Tantric Buddhism of Tibet*. Shambhala Publications, 2002.

Roberts, Peter Alan, trans. *Mahamudra and Related Instructions: Core Teachings of the Kagyu Schools*. Wisdom Publications, 2011.

Situ Rinpoche, Tai. *Tilopa: Some Glimpses Of His Life*. Dzalendara Publishing, 1988.

Styron, William. *Darkness Visible: A Memoir of Madness*. Vintage Classics, 1992.

Suzuki Roshi, Shunryu. *Zen Mind, Beginner's Mind: Informal Talks on Zen Meditation and Practice*. Weatherhill, 1973.

Trungpa Rinpoche, Chögyam. *The Collected Works of Chögyam Trungpa*. Shambhala Publications, 2004.

Trungpa Rinpoche, Chögyam. *The Pocket Chögyam Trungpa*. Shambhala Publications, 2017.

Trungpa Rinpoche, Chögyam, trans. *The Rain of Wisdom*. Shambhala Publications, 1999.

Tsangnyön Heruka. *The Life of Marpa the Translator*. Shambhala Publications, 1982.

Tulku Urgyen Rinpoche. *As It Is, Volume II*. Rangjung Yeshe Publications, 2004.

Tulku Urgyen Rinpoche. *Rainbow Painting*. Rangjung Yeshe Publications, 2004.

Waddell, Norman, trans. *Unborn: The Life and Teachings of Zen Master Bankei, 1622-1693*. North Point Press, 2000.

Thank you for reading *The Truth about Enlightenment*. We sincerely hope it benefits your spiritual journey.

To help readers along the path to enlightenment, we are offering you free exclusive material, including a treatise comparing the Mahamudra and Dzogchen enlightenment traditions.

To access this material, visit our website, fredhmeyermd.com. Look for the "Join our mailing list" link, and in the "How did you find us?" field enter: **READER**

We welcome your honest feedback on this book. Please share your thoughts through the retailer where you purchased it. Thank you!

Made in United States
Orlando, FL
15 November 2021